A Toolkit for Quantitative Data Analysis

Also by Sotirios Sarantakos

Data Analysis
Basic Stats Without Maths
Social Research (3rd edition)
Same-Sex Couples in Australia
Quality of Life in Rural Australia
Modern Families
Studying Modern Families
Troubled Children
Compendium of Social Research
Cohabitation in Transition
For a Caring Care
Living Together in Australia
Marriage and the Family
Die Atypische Familie

A Toolkit for Quantitative Data Analysis
Using SPSS

Sotirios Sarantakos

First published 2007 by
PALGRAVE MACMILLAN
Houndmills, Basingstoke, Hampshire RG21 6XS and
175 Fifth Avenue, New York, N.Y. 10010
Companies and representatives throughout the world

PALGRAVE MACMILLAN is the global academic imprint of the Palgrave
Macmillan division of St. Martin's Press, LLC and of Palgrave
Macmillan Ltd. Macmillan® is a registered trademark in the United
States, United Kingdom and other countries. Palgrave is a registered
trademark in the European Union and other countries.

ISBN-13: 978-0-230-50045-7
ISBN-10: 0-230-50045-5

This book is printed on paper suitable for recycling and made from
fully managed and sustained forest sources. Logging, pulping and
manufacturing processes are expected to conform to the
environmental regulations of the country of origin.

A catalogue record for this book is available from the British Library.

A catalog record for this book is available from the Library of Congress.

10   9   8   7   6   5   4   3   2   1
16 15 14 13 12 11 10 09 08 07

Printed in China

#85659601

To Sotirios Jr., Joshua and BJ.

Contents

About this book

This book is about how to conduct quantitative data analysis (QDA), using SPSS (version 15, as well as 10, 11, 12, 13 and 14). It focuses on the essence of data analysis (DA), and avoids unnecessary frills and long-winded jargon-based presentations. More specifically, this book:

- Employs a *simple* approach, making DA easily accessible to the novice.

- Is *free of maths and stats*: doing QDA requires neither mathematical skills nor statistical knowledge. Statistical tests are conducted by SPSS.

- Is *concise*: in about 100 pages it covers the essence of basic DA.

- Is *laconic*: it focuses on the essentials and offers only 'as much as necessary and as little as possible'.

- Is *systematic*: it follows a step-by-step, recipe-like approach that makes data analysis quick and easy, without sacrificing quality.

The focus of this book is primarily on data analysis and secondarily on statistics. In this sense, it focuses on how to conduct DA, namely on *which* tests to use and *how* to interpret the results. Simply, doing DA means: **focus** on an analytic task, **identify** the proper test, **open** the relevant page, **conduct** the test as instructed and **interpret** the results as advised.

This book is not a text but a guide. It does not introduce you to social research, its epistemological foundations or to the many philosophical or statistical conflicts and debates. It simply tells you how to handle the technical aspects of QDA in a simple but effective way, producing the outcomes required to answer research questions.

In this format, this book is a valuable guide to those who want to learn how to conduct basic QDA without long-winded descriptions and epistemological puzzles, and certainly a companion to students of sociology, psychology, health, education, journalism and social sciences in general, studying social research. It is also most useful to those who have some insight into the research process, who have access to data and who wish to conduct a quick, direct, easy and reliable QDA. In these cases, this book will be found to be most adequate, most reliable and most useful.

Sotirios Sarantakos
June 2007

Introduction

Data analysis (DA) is the process of transforming raw data to numbers, applying statistical tools, and aiming to describe, summarize and compare data, and to discover knowledge. This suggests that for an adequate and successful DA the researcher needs firstly data and secondly tools of DA.

What are data?

Data are basically pieces of information collected by the researcher before DA begins. They are answers to survey questions, responses to experimental stimuli, parts of texts, actions or behaviour options in a context of observation, reactions to situations within a focus group discussion, etc. Data are collected using methods such as experiments, content analysis and most of all through surveys, ie interviewing, and mail questionnaires. Quantitative versions of content analysis, observation and focus groups are also employed to gather data. These raw data are quantized and further prepared for analysis using coding.

What is coding?

Coding is the procedure of converting raw data into numbers, with each number representing a code and a code standing for a value or category. For instance, the answer 'Yes' becomes '1', 'I don't know' becomes '2', and 'No' becomes '3'. Also, 'Male' is substituted by the number '1'; and 'Female' by the number '2'. Hence, DA deals with the numbers which represent values or categories of variables.

What are variables?

Variables are empirical constructs that take more than one value. Gender is a variable; it contains the values 'male' and 'female'. Social class is another variable; it contains the values 'upper class', 'middle class' and 'lower class'. Age, finally, is another variable, which contains innumerable values, because it can be anything from 0 upwards, such as 7, 21, 25.3, 32.5 years, etc. Gender is a *nominal* variable; it names the categories it entails. Social class is an *ordinal* variable; it ranks its categories. Age is a *interval* variable; it contains values with equal intervals. An interval variable that also contains a zero as its starting point is a *ratio* variable.

In data analysis, variables are compared and interrelated with each other, and, depending on their position in the relationship, they can be independent or dependent variables. An *independent* variable is one that is assumed by the analyst to have an impact on another; the variable that is supposed to be affected by another is the *dependent* variable. In a study investigating the effects of religion on scholastic achievement, religion is the independent variable and scholastic achievement the dependent variable.

What are the types of DA?

There are two types of DA: *manual* and *electronic* (or computer-assisted) DA. DA is conducted predominantly using computers; this is why it is known as *computer assisted data analysis* (CADA). If the data are analysed manually, the analyst will begin the analysis immediately after coding. If, however, the analysis will be conducted electronically, the analyst will enter the data in the computer before analysis begins. In this guide we follow the second option.

What is the content of DA?

DA is statistical analysis, ie it is a procedure that uses statistical tests. Simply stated, the data analyst focuses on a research question and employs statistical tests to find an answer. The choice of tests is dictated by two factors, namely (a) the nature of the variables (ie whether they are nominal, ordinal, interval or ratio), and (b) the purpose of the analysis, eg whether it aims to describe distributions, to correlate variables, to compare groups, etc. There are different tests for nominal, ordinal and interval/ratio data, and also different tests for answering the various research questions (regarding correlation, inference, etc).

What are the outcomes of DA?

DA produces descriptions, estimates of central tendency, dispersion, correlation, regression and comparisons of groups. The results of statistical tests appear in the form of graphs, maps and tables, coefficients and other statistical symbols, all in many formats, as many and as diverse as the tests that produce them. Interpreting the outcomes of DA, ie making sense of the outcomes of the analysis, is the central task of the analyst.

What does interpretation entail?

During interpretation, analysts complete the path of data analysis, in a way turning back to the start of the research project. Whereas at the beginning of the study analysts converted words and meanings to numbers, at the last step of data analysis they turn numbers to words and meanings. Statistical interpretations are based on mathematical logic, and in this sense they are easy to construct, provided you know the rules of the game, eg the meaning of correlation coefficients and the power of significance tests and values. Nevertheless, making valid statements that are convincing and reflect real situations is another matter. And this is a point that deserves attention, for it is easy for the novice to exaggerate the value of the findings. For instance, there is a great difference between statistical significance and substantive significance – that is the practical importance of the findings for explanation, theory and social policy – and between correlation and causation.

What is the structure of DA?

In principle, DA is conducted in three steps: data entry, selection of an analytic task and statistical testing. (1) Data entry involves the transfer of data in the computer, providing in this way the material that is required for the computer-assisted data analysis. Although this procedure is indispensable, it usually is not considered a part of DA, and is normally completed before the actual analysis begins. (2) During the second step of data analysis researchers choose a specific task (analytic task) to focus their attention on, and decide *which* tests to employ, *when* and *why*. These tasks are listed in Table 1.1. (3) The third step is about running statistical tests, and focuses mainly on two tasks: (a) the mathematical computations, and (b) the interpretation of the mathematical symbols. The type of statistical tests employed in data analysis are shown in Table 1.1 and are conducted using SPSS.

What is SPSS?

SPSS is one out of many computer software programs employed by researchers and students when conducting CADA; SPSS stands for

Table 1.1 Analytic tasks and corresponding statistical tests

Analytic tasks	Corresponding test options
Describe graphically and/or numerically the distribution	Graphs: histograms, bar charts, pie charts Tables: frequency tables, crosstabs
Estimate central tendency	Mean, mode and median
Estimate dispersion	Standard deviation, range
Correlate variables	ϕ(phi) coefficient and Cramer's V, Somers' d, Lambda (λ) coefficient, Spearman's rho (ρ), and Pearson's r
Test predictions	Simple/multiple regression
Compare groups	Chi-square (χ^2); McNemar test; Wilcoxon test; t test; and analysis of variance.

Statistical Package for the Social Sciences. SAS and Minitab are another two popular programs but still, SPSS is the most common, particularly in the area of social sciences, and is available for Windows as well as for Mac OS X (SPSS 13).

SPSS is a dynamic, diverse and well integrated computer program, offering a variety of features and modules, tailored to meet the needs of its users. The basic version of SPSS focuses on data analysis but it offers a lot more, for instance it assists the planning of the study and data collection, data preparation and reporting. Put simply, this program contains all that is required for conducting a piece of research including quantitative data analysis, using a simple and easily accessible procedure.

Although all features of SPSS are useful, the central focus of most users is on data analysis, which not only offers a broad spectrum of options but also access to a powerful, fast, valid and reliable statistical analysis. This obviously is most useful to analysts with poor or no mathematical skills, but of equally great importance to those with statistical skills. There is no analyst nowadays who would conduct research and especially data analysis manually. Speed and reliability are two criteria that make CADA the only way even for the experienced statisticians. Access to a variety of forms of tabular and graphical presentation of the data and of reporting methods make SPSS even more practical and more useful for all users.

SPSS is available as a full program, or in a smaller version, the *Student Version*, specially tailored to the needs of the users. This is adequate and also less costly. For those who are interested in more complex procedures and multivariate techniques, *SPSS Advanced Models* is an appropriate extension. Advanced students may opt for *SPSS Graduate Pack* as an option; this includes the full version of SPSS Base, two add-on modules and, for Windows users, software for structural equation modelling (SEM). Also interesting are *SPSS Categories* and *SPSS Classification Trees* which introduce perceptual maps with optimal scaling and dimension reduction techniques as well as visual classification and decision trees.

A closer view of SPSS will be offered in the next section, where its major parts will be introduced.

Examples of online assistance

■ **Social research methods:**
www.socialresearchmethods.net/

■ **Online text:**
http://www.isixsigma.com/offsite.asp'A=Fr&Url=http://
nilesonline.com/stats/

■ **Glossaries:**
http://www.animatedsoftware.com/elearning/Statistics%20
Explained/glossary/se_glossary.html

http://stattrek.com/Help/Glossary.aspx

■ **Free statistical software:**
http://www.sixsigmalab.com/

CHAPTER 1

Getting to know your SPSS

SPSS – its many faces

As noted earlier, over the last ten years, SPSS appeared in a series of versions, of which 10, 11, 12, 13 and 14 are still employed by students; late in 2006, version 15 was published. Although each new version added important innovations and expansions, as far as basic statistics is concerned and with regard to the basic syntax files, versions 10–14 are almost identical. The same is true for version 15. The only area of basic statistics which requires slightly different commands is 'Graphs'. Improvement and expansion in this area offered additional options, and hence slight adjustments in the approach to charts are required.

In this volume, we shall use all versions and introduce the necessary instructions for each test used, but before we do that, let us get acquainted with the structure of SPSS for Windows, and particularly with the following:

- exploring SPSS for Windows
- Data Editor
- SPSS Viewer
- getting assistance.

After this introduction, we shall look at applying the program in data analysis, beginning with entering the data in the computer.

Exploring SPSS for Windows

What is this?

SPSS is a computer program used to carry out statistical tests for data analysis. In this guide we use SPSS versions 10–15.

The 'faces' of SPSS

When we work with SPSS, we are faced with a number of screens, namely the **Data Editor: Data View**, the **Data Editor: Variable View**, the **SPSS Viewer** and the **Statistics Coach**. These are the paths to the program and will be introduced after we explain a few 'tricks' that are used regularly when communicating with the computer.

Communicating with SPSS: abbreviated commands

Computers are instructed by means of commands: we use commands to instruct the commuter which test to compute and which aspects of each test to consider. We use also abbreviations of commands, by combining them in a sequence command. For instance, instead of using the commands 'Click A', and then 'Click B' and finally 'Click C', we may use 'Click A/B/C', or 'Go to A/B/C', or 'Choose A/B/C', etc. The following abbreviations are the most common.

- **Go to:** This suggests 'go to and click on'. Eg 'Go to Analyze' means go to Analyze and click on it.

- **Click:** This means press the left-hand side mouse button. For instance, 'Click on File' means point to and left-click on File. For pressing the right-hand side mouse button we use the command 'right-click'; eg 'right-click the chart'.

- **Activate:** This stands for click on the ○ or □ that stands before or after a specific word. For instance, 'Activate Pearson' means 'click on the sign that stands in front of Pearson'. When activated, these signs change to ⊙, ☑ or ☒.

- **Select** A/B/C/X or **Choose** A/B/C/X or **Click** A/B/C/X: These commands suggest to click on A, then on B, on C and on X successively. For instance, 'Select File/Open/Data' implies 'click File, then Open and then Data'.

■ **Transfer:** This command is used when a variable is to be moved from one box to another. Example: Transfer Gender to the Rows box. 'Transfer' means (1) highlight the variable in question and (2) click on the ▶ button on the right-hand side of the variables list.

Let us now get acquainted with the many 'faces' of SPSS.

Data Editor

What is this?

The Data Editor is the screen where you begin your work with SPSS. This is a spreadsheet-like system and appears in two forms, the **Data View** and the **Variable View**. You can toggle between them by clicking on either of the labels displayed at the bottom of the Data Editor screen. Data View and Variable View will be introduced briefly below.

Data View

The **Data Editor: Data View** is where the results of a study are entered and viewed. The screen here is arranged so that rows are assigned to cases and columns to variables. Each row contains the responses of one respondent to all questions; and each column contains the responses of all respondents to one variable. Rows are numbered; columns are named after their variable.

Variable View

The **Data Editor: Variable View** is where variables are defined, edited and viewed. In this editor, rows are for variables and columns are for variable attributes. The titles of the columns indicate the type of variable details that goes in the cells. These titles, their content and meaning, and some helpful hints as to how to fill in these cells are given below.

Name	Variable name; enter a name but do not use blanks, !, ?, ' or *. Also begin with a letter and do not end with a full stop.
Type	Data type; click on the shaded box to choose the right options.
Width	Column width; you may change it but often 8 is sufficient.
Decimals	Number of decimal places; set it according to need – usually 0.
Label	Variable labels; use labels up to 256 characters (eg 'subject's status').
Values	Set values and value labels, eg 1, 2 for men/women respectively.
Missing	Missing values; set it to 9 or 99 (usually 9).
Columns	Set columns to 8.
Align	Set alignment column contents to right, left or centre at will.
Measurement	Set to nominal, ordinal or scale (to be explained later).

As you see, some of the variable attributes are easy to define but others are not. More information on this will be given later in this section.

SPSS Viewer

What is this?

The SPSS Viewer (Figure 1.1) is where the output of statistical calculations (graphs, tables, etc) is displayed. It appears automatically after a statistical procedure is completed. Unlike the Data Editor, the SPSS Viewer does not contain rows and columns but two sections, the *outline pane* (narrow part, left) listing the titles of the computed tests, and the *contents pane* (wide part, right) where the actual output (eg tables, charts, etc) is stored and displayed.

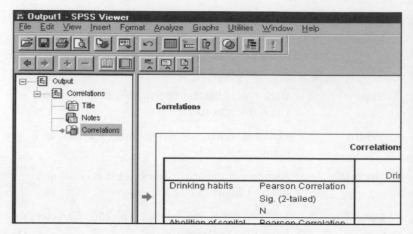

Figure 1.1

Briefly, the output of all tests conducted during one session are listed in the outline pane and are available for further study and comparisons in the content pane. When you click on an item, the corresponding output appears on the contents pane for inspection or further analysis.

The bar that divides the outline pane and the contents pane can be moved sideways at will. Just click on the bar, and while holding the mouse button down, move the pointer horizontally. The bar follows, adjusting the pane size as required. This is particularly necessary when long tables are displayed, too long for the standard-size pane. In such cases, shifting the bar accordingly allows a full display of the table.

Getting assistance

What is this?

SPSS provides a number of services geared towards making the use of the program easy and effective. Most interesting is the 'Tutorial' which offers step-by-step instructions on how to use the program. If you are interested in specific aspects of the program, the 'Statistics Coach' is very handy (Figure 1.2).

Getting to these sources of assistance is simple: Select **Help** and make your choice. If you choose the 'Statistics Coach', you come to the display shown in Figure 1.2 (SPSS 14), or to that shown in Figure 1.3 (SPSS 15).

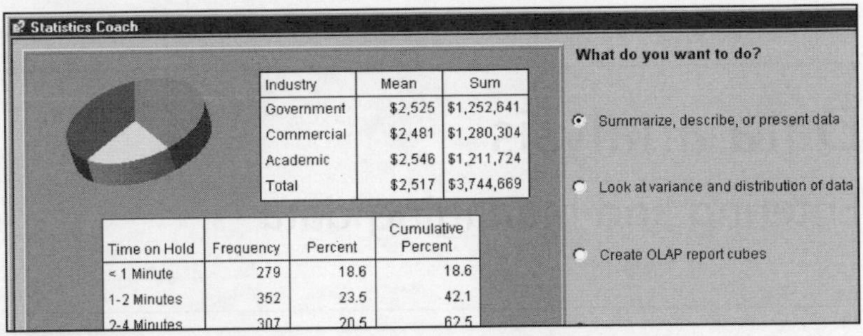

Figure 1.2

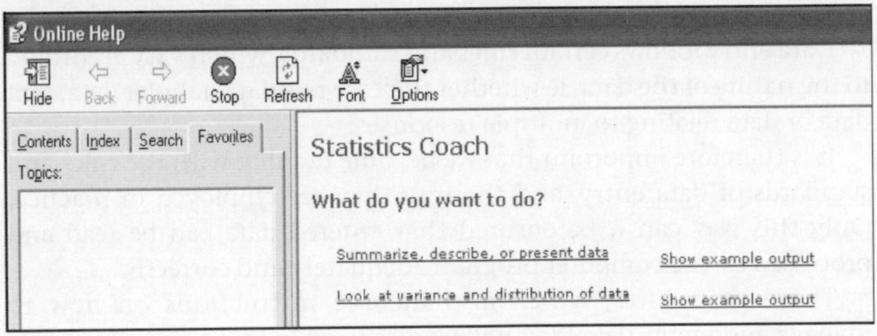

Figure 1.3

The search for specific aspects of analysis is very simple. In SPSS 15, for instance, you have a choice between set topics on the right-hand side and 'Contents', 'Index', 'Search' and 'Favourites' on the left-hand side. You find more than you expect to find in a computer program.

CHAPTER 2

Data analysis
Entering and managing data

As noted earlier the process of CADA begins after the research findings are entered in the computer. Data entry is the first step towards CADA.

Data entry follows certain rules and standards, which vary according to the nature of the data, ie whether they are raw data, tabular data, text data or data relating to multiple responses.

It is therefore important that we become familiar with the rules and standards of data entry, and the way they are employed in practice. Only this way can it be ensured that entered data can be read and processed by the computer program adequately and correctly.

These procedures, which also include instructions on how to manage and merge data files, will be discussed in this chapter.

> **Remember!**
> Social research is guided by scientific principles and by statistical standards. In addition, researchers follow ethical standards in all steps of the research process. This is particularly so when employing CADA, where a degree of 'detachment' of the researcher from the data is possible or even inevitable. For the researcher, adherence to ethical principles is a personal commitment and a professional requirement.

Entering raw data

Introduction

Raw data are unprocessed data, ie they are as gathered by the researcher. Such data have no format or structure of the kind the computer program can identify and recognize. For this reason, there is a need to prepare the program so that entered data can be recognized, sorted, stored and processed by the system adequately. This is accomplished by what we know as 'defining' the variables.

Following this, the process of entering raw data in the computer is conducted in two steps. These are:

- defining the variables

- data entry.

These steps will be explained briefly next.

1. Defining variables

Why define variables?
As noted above, the purpose of defining the variables is to set in the system the names and attributes of the variables, so that data entered in the computer are automatically recognized, sorted out and distributed by the program accordingly.

How to do it
To define a variable we proceed as follows:

- Go to **SPSS Data Editor** and click on **Variable View** (bottom left).

- Go to the first row.

- Enter in the columns the required information (name, type, etc of the variable).

- Repeat process for second and subsequent variables.

Helpful hints:

- Set the options in each column by clicking the shaded square or hit the (up/down) arrow.

- Leave **width**, **column** and **align** unchanged.

- Set **missing** to 9; if you have more than nine response categories in your questions, set it to 99, and to 999 if you have more than 99 response categories.

- Set **measure** as required. The options, as given in the SPSS User's Guide, are explained below. If you are entering a:
  - string (alphanumerical) variable: **Set to nominal**
  - string and numeric variable with defined value labels: **Set to ordinal**
  - numeric variable without defined value labels but less than a specified number of unique values: **Set to ordinal**
  - numeric variables without defined value labels and more than a specified number of unique values: **Set to scale.**

An example
In the following we shall demonstrate how to define the variable SEX. To accomplish this, we proceed as follows:

1 In the SPSS Data Editor **click on** 'Variable View' (at the bottom of the screen).

2 **Go to** the first column, first line of the screen, and type in the column 'Name' the word 'Sex'.

3 **Move** to 'Type', click on the shaded box and set the type to 'numeric'.

4 **Move** to 'Width' and leave it at 8; this is adequate.

5 **Move** to 'Decimals' and change it to 0, by clicking on the arrow that points down.

6 **Move** to 'Label' and type in the full name of the variable, eg Sex of Subjects.

7 **Move** to 'Values' and click on the shaded box next to it.

- In the box 'Value' type '1' (the code for 'Male').

- Move to 'Value label', type 'Male' and then click 'Add'.

- Return to 'Value' and type '2' (for Female).

- Go to 'Value label', and type 'Female'.

- Click 'Add' and then 'OK'.

8 **Move** to 'Missing' and click on the shaded box. In the new window:

- activate 'Discrete missing values'

- type '9' in the 'Discrete missing values' box; and click OK.

9 **Move** to 'Columns', and set the width to 8.

10 **Move** to 'Align' and leave it as is (right), or set as you wish.

11 **Move** to 'measure' and change it to 'nominal'.

The variable SEX has now been defined, and the computer is ready to define additional variables. The Data Editor screen will read as shown in Figure 2.1. We then move to the second row and enter the second variable, following the same steps we used previously. The remaining variables are entered the same way.

2. Entering the data

Introduction
We demonstrate data entry using the seven variables shown below, which are part of a longer survey. The response categories are also included.

- **sex** (Male –1; Female –2)

- **drinking habits** (Drinking a lot –1; Drinking socially –2; Not drinking at all –3)

- **type of car owned** (Japanese –1; European –2; US –3; Other –4)

- **marital status** (Single –1; Married –2; Divorced/separated –3; Widowed –4)

- **gay marriage**; Are you in favour of gay marriage? (Strongly in favour –5; In favour –4; No opinion –3; Against –2; Strongly against –1)

- **capital punishment**; Are you in favour of capital punishment? (Strongly in favour –5; In favour –4; No opinion –3; Against –2; Very much against –1)

- **drug shooting galleries**; Are you in favour of having drug shooting galleries? (Strongly in favour –5; In favour –4; No opinion –3; Against –2; Very much against –1).

	Name	Type	Width	Decimals	Label	Values	Missing	Columns	Align	Measure
1	sex	Numeric	8	0	Sex of subjects	{1, male}...	9	8	Right	Nominal
2										
3										
4										
5										

Figure 2.1

The variables have already been defined as explained earlier, and their names appear at the top of the columns. The responses to the questions (ie the data) are to be entered in the computer for processing (Figure 2.1).

How to do it

To enter the data in the computer we go to Data Editor: Data View and type in the first line of the screen one-by-one the answers of the first respondent given to each of the seven questions, placing each answer under the corresponding variable name. For instance, if the answers of the first respondent to the seven questions were as follows

Qu1 – 1 Qu2 – 3 Qu3 – 1 Qu4 – 1 Qu5 – 5 Qu6 – 1 Qu7 – 1

we would type 1 under variable 'sex', 3 under 'drinking', 1 under 'car', and so on, setting one number in each column. If the answers of the second respondent to the questions were 2, 2, 2, 3, 2, 2, 2, respectively, we would type them the same way. The answers of the first 18 respondents, entered in the computer this way, are as shown in Figure 2.2.

Now the data are in the computer, and can be subjected to any statistical tests that researchers consider appropriate.

Entering tabular data

What is this?

This is about how to enter in the computer data contained in a table. Such data cannot be processed using the method reported in the previous section.

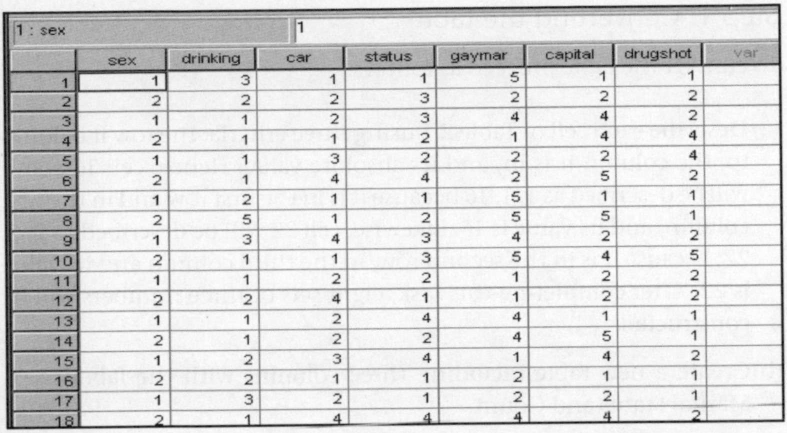

1 : sex 1

	sex	drinking	car	status	gaymar	capital	drugshot	var
1	1	3	1	1	5	1	1	
2	2	2	2	3	2	2	2	
3	1	1	2	3	4	4	2	
4	2	1	1	2	1	4	4	
5	1	1	3	2	2	2	4	
6	2	1	4	4	2	5	2	
7	1	2	1	1	5	1	1	
8	2	5	1	2	5	5	1	
9	1	3	4	3	4	2	2	
10	2	1	1	3	5	4	5	
11	1	1	2	2	1	2	2	
12	2	2	4	1	1	2	2	
13	1	1	2	4	4	1	1	
14	2	1	2	2	4	5	1	
15	1	2	3	4	1	4	2	
16	2	2	1	1	2	1	1	
17	1	3	2	1	2	2	1	
18	2	1	4	4	4	4	2	

Figure 2.2

Example

A researcher wishes to analyse the data contained in Table 2.1. It is therefore necessary to enter the data in the computer.

Table 2.1 Gender by marital status

Sex	Single	Married	Divorced	Widowed
Males	16	115	21	14
Females	11	101	22	32

How to do it

Entering tabular data follows three distinct steps. These are:

1 Converting the table into one showing the place of the cells within the table; and the numerical value of each cell.

2 Defining the variables.

3 Entering the data.

These steps will be explained next.

Step 1: Converting the table

To convert the table proceed as follows:

(a) **Describe** each cell of Table 2.1 using three criteria: the row it belongs to, the column it is in, and its absolute value. Hence, cell 16 above will be described as 1, 1, 16 because it is in the first row and in the first column, and its value is 16. Likewise, cell 22 will be described as 2, 3, 22, because it is in the second row, in the third column and its value is 22. After completing this task, eight sets of three numbers will be constructed.

(b) **Create** a new table including three columns with the labels: Sex, Marital Status and Count.

(c) **Set** the first of the three numbers of each set in the column 'Sex', the second in the column 'Marital status' and the third in the column 'Count'. Repeat this process for the remaining sets. When this procedure is completed, the table will be as shown in Table 2.2.

Table 2.2 Converted table

Sex	Marital status	Count
1	1	16
1	2	115
1	3	21
1	4	14
2	1	11
2	2	101
2	3	22
2	4	32

Step 2: Define the variables

Define the variables: **Sex**, entailing males (1) and females (2); **Status** (for Marital status), containing the four categories: single (1), married (2), divorced (3) widowed (4); and **Count**, which requires no further details. Finally, set 'Sex' and 'Status' to 'Nominal' and 'Count' to 'Scale'. Following this, the names of the three variables will appear at the top of the first three columns of the screen (Figure 2.3).

	sex	status	count	var	var
1	1	1	16		
2	1	2	115		
3	1	3	21		
4	1	4	14		
5	2	1	11		
6	2	2	101		
7	2	3	22		
8	2	4	32		
9					
10					
11					

Figure 2.3

Step 3: Enter the data

To enter the data of the new table in the computer, transfer the data of the table column 'sex' to the column 'sex' of Data Editor. Repeat this process for the remaining columns of the table. The Data Editor screen will look as shown above. Data entry is now complete and we can proceed with the analysis.

To ensure that you entered the data correctly, you may compute a crosstabulation of the two variables asking for a 'crosstab'. To obtain a crosstab you proceed as follows:

- Go to **Analyze/Descriptive Statistics/Crosstabs**.
- Transfer **Sex** to **Row(s)** box; and **Status** to **Column(s)** box.
- Go to **Data/Weight cases**, and activate **Weight cases by**.
- Transfer **Count** to **Frequency variable:** box.
- Click **OK**, and again **OK**.

The content of the table in the output should be as shown in Figure 2.4, which is the original table.

If the table in the output is different, check your details and repeat the procedure; you must have made a mistake.

Sex of subjects * Status of subjects Crosstabulation

Count

		Status of subjects				Total
		single	married	divorced	widowed	
Sex of subjects	male	16	115	21	14	166
	female	11	101	22	32	166
Total		27	216	43	46	332

Figure 2.4

Entering text data files

What is this?

This is about entering in the computer text (ASCII) data, which often include hundreds of variables and thousands of cases. Apart from their nature, their size makes the use of any other entry procedure extremely time-consuming. The set of data below is a small part of such a file, and alos contains variable names. Each line represents a case.

Table 2.3

sex	id	sta	tst	..	..	..
1	22	31	2	..	..	..
2	21	24	9	..	..	..
1	31	12	8	..	..	..

How to do it

The procedure for entering text data proceeds as follows.

- Select **File** and then click on **Read Text Data** and open the text file.

- In the new window activate **No** and click on **Next**.

- In the new window activate **Delimited** and **Yes** and click on **Next**.

- In the new window set **First case of data begins** to **2**.

- Activate **Each line represents** and **All of the cases** and click on **Next**.

- Activate the delimiter you use (tab, comma, etc.) – in our case **Tab** and click **Next**.

- Leave window as is and click on **Next** and then on **Finish**.

The selected text file is now entered as intended (see Figure 2.5). It is worth noting that if text data do not include variable names, the data entry procedure is slightly different. Such cases are however not very common.

	sex	id	sta	tst	var	var	var	var	var
1	1	22.0	31.0	2					
2	2	21.0	24.0	9					
3	1	31.0	12.0	8					
4									

Figure 2.5

Entering data with multiple responses

What is this?

Earlier we explained how to enter data obtained using multiple-choice questions. Here we want to know how to enter responses to multiple-response questions. The difference between the two is that in the former we could give only one answer (eg male or female); in the latter, we can give more than one answer. This is the case, for instance, when asked to state the types of books you usually read in the library, such as sociology, psychology, history books, etc, where more than one option can be ticked. In such cases the process of entering multiple responses in the computer follows a different path.

Example

A youth worker inquired about the kind of leisure time activities 100 young people pursued during their free time. The questionnaire contained the following multiple-response set, offering respondents the option to tick as many boxes as they consider appropriate.

- TV watching
- sport
- music
- movies
- other.

How do we enter multiple responses to the computer? What are the appropriate procedures?

How to do it

The path of data entry here contains two steps: the first is to **define the variables**, and the second to **define multiple response sets**. We shall show this procedure using the above example.

Step 1: Define the variables

To define the variables you do the following:

1 **Convert the response categories into variables.** Here the variable 'Leisure time activities' will be converted into five separate variables, namely TV watching, sport, music, movies and other.

2 **Define the new variables in the computer.** This implies defining the five variables as explained earlier, by going to Variable View and setting name, width, etc.

3 **Set values for each of these variables** to 0 for No (not pursuing this type of leisure) and to 1 for Yes (for pursuing it).

4 **Enter the responses for each variable in the Data View.** The ticked options will be given an '1', and those not ticked will be given a '0'. For instance, the entries for a male respondent who ticked the first, third and fifth option will be as shown in the first line of the output shown in Figure 2.6 (1, 0, 1, 0 and 1).

	TV	Sport	Music	Movies	Other	var	var	var
1	1	0	1	0	1			
2	0	1	1	1	1			
3	1	1	0	0	1			
4	0	0	1	1	1			
5	1	1	0	1	1			
6	1	1	1	0	1			
7	1	0	0	0	1			
8	1	1	1	0	1			
9	1	0	0	1	1			
10	1	1	1	0	1			
11	1	0	1	0	1			
12	1	0	0	1	1			
13	0	1	1	1	1			
14	1	0	0	0	1			
15	1	1	1	1	1			
16								

Figure 2.6

Following the procedure described above and using a set of corresponding hypothetical data, the results of these 15 respondents, set in the computer, will be as shown in Figure 2.6.

Step 2: Defining multiple response sets

The second step of entering multiple responses is to instruct the computer that the new variables belong together. This proceeds as follows:

- Select **Analyze/Multiple Response/Define Variable sets**.

- Transfer the five variables to the **Variables in Set** box.

- Activate **Dichotomies** and type **1** in the **Counted value** box.

- Type **Leisure** in the **Name** box (a name for the set that includes the new variables).

- Type **Leisure time activities** in the **Label** box.

- Click **Add** (this adds the multiple response set to the list of defined sets).

After completing these steps, the computer will integrate the variables set above in the 'Variables in Set' box into one set, and add the multiple response set to the list of defined sets. The name of the multiple response set is marked by the sign $ ($leisure) and is ready for further analysis.

It must be noted that, as advised by SPSS during the process of analysis, sets defined here 'are only available in the Multiple response Frequencies and Crosstabs procedure. Use Define Multiple Response Sets on the Data menu for sets used elsewhere.'

Managing SPSS files

Changing the content (cut, copy, paste)

SPSS files can be managed like Word files. They or their parts (eg cells, columns or rows) can be deleted/cut, copied or pasted as Word files. The common path to follow is

- Go to **Data Editor: Data View** and open the file.
- Highlight the part in question (cell, column or row).
- Go to **Edit** and select the desired function (copy, cut or paste).

Changing the content of cells is even easier. Just highlight the cell, and type in the new value. Likewise, a column or row can be copied/cut and pasted using similar procedures.

Inserting rows and columns

To insert a new (empty) row (case):

- Highlight the row above which you wish to insert the new one.
- Go to **Data** and click on **Insert Case**.

To insert a new (empty) column (variable):

- Highlight the column at the right of which you intend to insert the new column.

- Go to **Data** and click on **Insert column**.

Saving SPSS data

To save SPSS files you proceed as follows.

- Go to File/Save as and choose the location where the file is to be saved.
- Type the file name in the name box, (eg study1.sav) and click OK.

Loading SPSS files

SPSS files can be retrieved by following the procedures employed in word processing. For instance, to retrieve a file you proceed as follows.

- Select **File/Open/Data**.
- Highlight the SPSS file you wish to retrieve, and click **OK**.

Following this, the file is loaded

Loading Spreadsheet or Database files

SPSS reads almost all popular files, eg SYSTAT, Excel, Lotus 1-2-3, SYLK and dBase. The path of loading such data is similar to that used for SPSS files, eg **File/Open Database/New Query** – unless you wish to edit a saved query, in which case the last command is 'Edit Query'. You then choose the data source and file; the Database Wizard will lead you through the process of loading the desired files.

Merging SPSS files

In SPSS you can merge two files into one, as long as they entail the same variables. This is the case, for instance, when data collection and data entry were undertaken by two (or more) researchers, using the same research instruments, variables, etc, and the data are available in two files. To merge two SPSS files you proceed as follows:

- Open the old file (base file) to which the new file is to be added.

- Go to **Data/Merge files/Add cases**.

- Select the new file to be added to the base file.

- Click on **Open** and then click **OK** (this will merge the two data sets).

The two files are now merged into one. To add another file to the new file, repeat the steps shown above, using the newly created file as the base file.

It should be noted that if the file to be added uses names for the value labels, codes etc that are different from those used in the base file, the value labels, codes etc of the base file will be applied. If the base file contains no such information (eg value names, names of value labels), those of the new file will be applied.

Remember!

Ethics has become an integral part and a compulsory require-ment of scientific social research. Ethical requirements refer predominantly to the protection of participants but also to the quality of research outcomes. In this context, deception, dishon-esty, fraud, misconduct and cheating are not acceptable. In most cases these ethical issues refer to data collection but they must also be considered with regard to data analysis.

Some of the areas of DA in which ethical standards are expected to be observed are bias in choosing (a) the data for analysis, (b) the analytic tasks, and (c) the statistical tests, as well as (d) in interpreting the data, and (e) in reporting the findings. It is unethical, for instance, to manipulate procedures and results for personal reasons: for example, in order to support and 'prove' personal views, or to conceal findings that do not support personal views and beliefs.

CHAPTER 3

Transforming data

In this chapter we shall introduce a few useful statistical techniques which are often thought to be less commonly used by, and beyond the range of, the novice. Be that as it may, they are a central part of CADA and deserve our attention. They are the following:

- recoding reverse scale items
- recoding multiple responses
- getting random samples
- getting sub-groups
- collapsing numeric variables
- creating composite variables.

Some of these methods allow the analyst to convert the structure of SPSS data into a different format that allows further analysis. Others help to reorganize the data so that specific groups of data can be addressed separately.

Recoding reverse scale items

What is this?

This procedure is used to reorganize reverse scale items so that they are in tune with the other items of the scale. But, what are reverse scale items? Let us explain this. Consider the questions in Table 3.1.

Both questions explore a person's attitude to life, with question (1) employing a positive and with question (2) employing a negative approach. A man who is very happy with his life will answer question (1) by ticking 'Strongly agree' and will be given a score of 5; but

27

Table 3.1

(1) I am very happy with my life	(2) My life is nothing but a misery
(5) Strongly agree	(5) Strongly agree
(4) Agree	(4) Agree
(3) Undecided	(3) Undecided
(2) Disagree	(2) Disagree
(1) Strongly disagree	(1) Strongly disagree

responding to question (2) he will tick 'Strongly disagree' and be given a score of 1.

In this sense, the same attitude to life is expressed by 5 in one case and by 1 in the other; hence, 5 and 1 express the same attitude. Likewise, 5 in question (1) has a different meaning from a 5 given in question (2). This means that, considering the standard arrangement of scale items, in question (2) the items are numbered in reverse; ie question (2) contains *reverse items*, and if they are left unchanged they will cause serious errors when the scores are added up and evaluated.

For this reason, response sets with reverse items are marked by an (R) in the questionnaire, and before computations are conducted, the response categories are recoded so that their values are consistent with all other items of the scale. For instance, 5 becomes 1, 4 becomes 2, 3 remains the same, 2 is converted to 4, and 1 becomes 5.

Obviously, you can take the easy way and adjust the reverse items before entering them in the computer. But there are cases where scores are entered in the computer in their original form; this makes recoding necessary. We should also remember that there are cases where surveys are conducted electronically, and questionnaires are only available through the computer, where respondents answer the questions, and the responses are automatically loaded in the system.

Below we show how to instruct the computer to recode reverse items.

How to recode reverse scale items

To recode the scale of the second question above, we open the file and proceed as follows:

- Select **Transform/Recode/Into Same Variables**.

- Transfer **Attitude** to **Numeric Variables** box.

- Click on **Old and New Values**.

- In the **Old Value** section activate **Value** and type **1** in it.

- In the **New Value** section activate **Value**, type **5** in it, and click on **Add**.

- In the **Old Value** section activate **Value** and type **2** in it.

- In the **New Value** section activate **Value**, type **4** in it, and click on **Add**.

- In the **Old Value** section activate **Value** and type **4** in it.

- In the **New Value** section activate **Value**, type **2** in it, and click on **Add**.

- In the **Old Value** section activate **Value** and type **5** in it.

- In the **New Value** section activate **Value**, type **1** in it, and click on **Add**.

  NOTE: Given that **3** remains the same, it is not recoded.

- Click on **Continue** and then **OK**.

Upon completion of these steps, the scale with the reverse items is recoded and the variables redefined. Note that more than one variable can be recoded simultaneously.

Caution
When recoding a scale, the computer does not add a new variable to the file. It rather recodes the old variable in the matrix, and the variable with the old codes is replaced by the new. Hence, if you wish to retain the original variable, you have to make relevant arrangements.

Recoding multiple responses

What is this?

This is a procedure that is used when the researcher wishes to change the codes of the responses of multiple-choice questions. It is, used, for instance, when the researcher wants to reduce the number of the responses, say, from five to three.

An example

A researcher wishes to reduce the responses 'Non-drinkers' (1); 'Social drinkers' (2); and 'Compulsive drinkers' (3) to 'Non-drinkers' (1) and 'Drinkers' (2), by collapsing the last two responses into one, and by assigning it the value 'Drinkers' and the code 2. The first response retains the old value and code.

How to recode

The process of converting a variable into another is similar to that introduced in the previous section, and is referred to in the SPSS procedures as 'Recoding'. Using the example referred to above as explained, ie reducing the responses from three to two, while retaining the status of the first response, and by collapsing responses 2 and 3 to one under 'Drinkers' (2), we proceed as follows.

- **V.15**: Select **Transform/Recode Into different variables**.

- **V.14**: Select **Transform/Recode/Into different variables**.

- Transfer **Drinking** to **Input Variable->Output Variable** box.

- Enter the new name **Drinkers** in the **Output variable** box.

- Click on **Old and New Values**.

- Type **1** in the **Old Value/Value** box and **1** in the **New Value/Value** box.

- Type **2** in the **Old Value/Value** box and **2** in the **New Value/Value** box.

- Type **3** in the **Old Value/Value** box and **2** in the **New Value/Value** box.

- Click on **Continue** and then **OK**.

- Go to **Variable View** and set values to reflect the new categories.

  (**1** for non-drinkers and **2** for drinkers)

This process changes the old variable into a new one which will either replace the old variable or create an additional variable. If you wish to create a new variable and delete the old one, in your first step, instead of choosing 'Into different variables' use 'Into same variables'. Using the option 'Into different variables' is a better choice because this way you retain the old variable data.

Getting random samples

What is this?

This is about a procedure that enables the researcher to obtain random samples from a large set of data already entered in the computer, and to focus the analysis on these samples. One reason for this is to select a representative sample and subject the respondents to a more focused in-depth analysis.

How to do it

There are two ways of obtaining random samples. One uses percentages and the other uses absolute numbers as a guide. In the former we draw a sample that contains a certain percentage of all cases, eg 10%. In the latter we construct the random sample so that it contains a specific number of cases, say 500 or 5000.

In technical terms, when the computer selects the sample, it blocks out the cases that are to be excluded from the sample, and allows access only to cases that belong to the random sample. This is visually displayed in the file through a slash on the ID number of the excluded cases. We shall introduce both methods below.

1 Using percentages as a guide

If we want to obtain a random sample containing 25% of a large SPSS file we proceed as follows:

- Open a data file that is to be sampled.

- Go to **Data/Select cases**.

- Activate **Random sample of cases**.

- Click on **Sample**.

- In the new window activate **Approximately**.

- Enter **25** in the **% of all Cases** box (since we want a 25% sample).

- Click on **Continue**.

- Click **OK**.

The outcome of the sample selection is shown in the output displayed in the next page. This display contains the original cases and variables, only the ID number of the cases that are excluded from the random sample is crossed out ('filtered out'); they make up 75% of all cases. The excluded items are still in the file and can be restored but until then access to them is not available. The remaining 25% of the cases, which are not crossed out, constitute the random sample. Any computations that will be undertaken after this point in time will refer only to the remaining 25% of the original cases, ie to the random sample. See Figure 3.1.

2 Using absolute numbers as a guide

The second method of obtaining random samples is identical to that described above, only in order to determine the size of the sample it uses not percentages but absolute numbers. Instead of setting the random sample size to 25% of the cases, we set it to, say, 340 cases. To obtain a random sample containing 340 of the 10,000 cases we proceed as follows.

	id	sex	drinking	car	status
1	1	1	3	1	1
2	2	2	2	2	3
3	3	1	1	2	3
4	4	2	1	1	2
5	5	1	1	3	2
6	6	2	1	4	4
7	7	1	2	1	1
8	8	2	3	1	2
9	9	1	3	4	3

Figure 3.1

- Open the data file that is to be sampled.

- Select **Data/Select cases**.

- Activate **Random sample of cases** and click on **Sample**.

- In the new window activate **Exactly**.

- Type **340** in the box on the left, and **10000** in the box on the right.

  (This means 'take 340 of the 10000 cases'.)

- Click **Continue** and then **OK**.

The output is similar to the one obtained using percentages, and is interpreted the same way.

Getting sub-groups

What is this?

This is about a procedure which enables the researcher to analyse parts (sub-groups) of a variable already entered in the computer. In technical terms, this extracts a sub-group from a variable and constructs a new variable that contains the data of the sub-group only.

Example

Applied in the case of the variable 'Gender', if the researcher wishes to focus the analysis on 'Males' only, using the information contained in the variable 'Gender', this procedure creates a new variable that contains data for 'Males' only. In the following we shall demonstrate how this is facilitated.

How to do it

To construct a variable that contains the category 'Males' from the variable 'Gender' we proceed as follows:

- Select **Data/Select cases**.

- Activate **If condition is satisfied** and click on **If**.

- Transfer **Gender** to the box on the right and type next to it =**1** (ie Gender=1).

  (Meaning: arrange that gender has only one category, namely 'males'.)

- Click **Continue** and then **OK**.

Following this, the SPSS Viewer displays the output shown in Figure 3.2.

What does this mean?

This shows that the code 2 in the ID column (standing for 'Female') has been crossed out, and a new variable ('filter_$') is constructed and added next to the existing list of variables. This variable contains the codes 1, for Males, and 0, for Females, meaning that they are excluded from the list. Consequently, any analytic procedure that follows this arrangement will refer to males only.

If the analysis were to focus on females only, the same path would be followed as described above, except that, in step 3, instead of typing =**1**, we insert =**2**. Following this, any computations of variables will refer to females only.

The procedure of obtaining variables for sub-groups does not delete or change the original variable in any way. To restore the variable, the same path described above will be followed, only in step 3 we

	Attitudes	Gender	filter_$	var	var	var
1	1	1	1			
2	1	2	0			
3	1	2	0			
4	1	2	0			
5	2	2	0			
6	2	2	0			
7	2	2	0			
8	2	2	0			
9	2	1	1			
10	2	1	1			
11	3	1	1			
12	3	1	1			
13	3	1	1			
14	3	2	0			
15	3	2	0			

Figure 3.2

transfer the variable 'Gender' to the box, without inserting =1 or =2 next to it.

Collapsing numeric variables

What is this?

This is a procedure that enables the researcher to collapse numeric (continuous) variables and convert them to categorical variables. For instance, it can convert test scores ranging from 1 to 10 to 'Pass' or 'Fail'. In this section we shall see how this procedure is facilitated.

Example

In an attitude study of 200 rural residents, the age of the participants was found to range from 16 to 95. After examining the findings, it was decided to evaluate the responses according to whether respondents were 'Old', 'Middle aged' or 'Young'. Hence, the variable is to be redefined so that the age scores are collapsed into three age groups.

How to compute it

Before starting the procedure we need to specify the boundaries of the age groups; we set them to 16–45 for 'Young', 46–75 for 'Middle-aged', and 76–95 for 'Old'. Having established these parameters, we proceed as follows.

- Select **Transform/Recode/Into Different Variables**.

- Transfer **Age** to the **Numeric Variable -> Output Variable** box.

- Type a new variable name (**Age_cat**) and a new **label**, in the boxes under **Name** and **Label** respectively.

- Click **Change** (the new name is added next to the old name).

- Click on **Old and New Values**.

- Activate the top **Range** and in the first box type **16** (the lowest age recorded), and in the next box **45**, being the top age for this group.

- Activate **Value** in the **New Value** window section and type **1** in the empty box (being the value for **Young**).

- Click on **Add**.

- Activate the top **Range** and in the first box type **46** (the bottom age limit of this group) and in the next box type **75**, which is the top age value for this group.

- Activate **Value** in the **New Value** window section and type **2** in the empty box (This is the value for the **Middle-aged**).

- Click on **Add**.

- Activate the top **Range** and in the first box type **76** (the bottom limit of this group), and in the next box **95**, which is the top age recorded in the study.

- Activate **Value** in the **New Value** window section and type **3** in the empty box (this is the value for **Old**).

- Click **Add** and **Continue**.

- Click **OK**.

An image of the output on Viewer is shown in Figure 3.3.

This output shows the respondents ID (47–60), the numerical age of each respondent and the new variable 'age_cat' as instructed, with 1 standing for 'Young', 2 for 'Middle-aged' and 3 for 'Old'. In this part of the data all are young. However, all cases in this file have their age

	age	age_cat	var	var	var	var	var	var
47	28	1.00						
48	37	1.00						
49	36	1.00						
50	37	1.00						
51	28	1.00						
52	19	1.00						
53	22	1.00						
54	19	1.00						
55	24	1.00						
56	19	1.00						
57	22	1.00						
58	26	1.00						
59	38	1.00						
60	15	1.00						

Figure 3.3

converted from a number to a category (young, middle-aged and old) expressed in a number between 1 and 3, and every procedure under-taken in this file will treat age as a categorical variable. Remember, the original numeric variable ('age') is still intact!

By the way
Do you think that the decimal points in the new variable are necessary? I don't think so! You can delete them by going to Variable View and setting decimals to zero.

Creating composite variables

What is this?

This is a procedure employed to construct a composite variable, namely one that contains a summary of several variables. The new variable integrates all variables including their responses into one unit. For instance, a scale on wellbeing may contain several questions, one on social wellbeing, another on emotional wellbeing, and another on physical health, each containing a score. A composite variable (say, 'wellbeing') will substitute the single questions and assume their scores in one unit. We shall see in this section how to create such variables.

An example

The scale on family wellbeing contains a set of 5 variables, ie fam_01, fam_02, fam_03, fam_04 and fam_05. Now we wish to integrate the responses to these five variables into one new summary variable (famscore). This allows the researcher to contrast and crosstabulate 'famscore' with other variables, facilitating in this way a more accurate assessment of the role of this factor within several contexts.

How to do it

To construct a composite variable we proceed as follows:

- Select **Transform** and click on **Compute** [or **Compute variable**].

- Type the name of the new variable **famscore** in the **Target Variable** box.

- Transfer **fam_01** to the **Numeric Expression** box, and click on the + button.

- Transfer **fam_02** to the **Numeric Expression** box, and click on the + button.

- Transfer **fam_03** to the **Numeric Expression** box, and click on the + button.

- Transfer **fam_04** to the **Numeric Expression** box, and click on the + button.

- Transfer **fam_05** to the **Numeric Expression** box.

- Click **OK**.

During this process, the computer collapsed these variables into one, added the responses to each response category together, and assigned the summary value to response to the new variable 'famscore'. When this procedure is completed, the composite variable is constructed, and can be treated as any other variable. The researcher can now address family wellbeing like any other variable, and explore interrelationships within the parameters of statistical analysis.

CHAPTER 4

Tables, central tendency and dispersion

After the data have been entered in the computer and relevant adjustments and transformations have been made, the door is open to task-related data analysis. Here the analyst begins asking questions and looks for answers. The first question that is usually addressed at the beginning of DA is about detailed information regarding specific trends in the data, as well as an accurate description of general trends in and the shape of the distribution. More specifically, the central items on which the analyst will focus at this stage of the analysis are:

- tables, such as frequency tables and crosstabs
- mean, mode, and median
- standard deviation
- Z scores
- statistics for sub-groups.

Tables offer information about one, two or more variables. Mean, mode and median tell us about the most common trends in the data; standard deviation describes the spread of the data; and Z scores offer a way of standardizing certain forms of research output. Getting measures for parts or sub-groups of variables is another interesting and useful procedure employed at the start of DA.

These are the issues that will be addressed in this chapter, including their nature, application and computation.

As noted above, tables are used to present a summary of the main results of the study, in a rather general and descriptive manner. Tables may tell us how age is spread among the respondents; whether the number of religious men is larger than that of religious women; or whether middle-aged women earn more than young men. More specifically, tables can be univariate, describing one variable, bivariate, describing two variables, or multivariate, describing more than two variables. SPSS addresses tabular presentation of findings using the terms 'frequency tables' and 'crosstabs'. We employ also these terms and begin our discussion with the former.

Frequency tables

What are they?

Frequency tables summarize data, contain one variable only, and as the name indicates, describe frequencies.

How to obtain frequency tables

To construct a frequency table, say for 'Attitudes to euthanasia', like that shown in Figure 4.1 you proceed as follows:

- Select **Analyze/Descriptive Statistics/ Frequencies**.
- Transfer **Attitudes** to **Variable(s)** box.
- Activate **Display frequency tables** and click **OK**.

Following this, the Viewer displays the table shown in the figure. In fact, you could have instructed the computer to provide more information, eg by clicking on 'Charts', after transferring the variable to the variable(s) box, and choosing an option.

What does this mean?

The table displays count and percentage for each of the response options (under 'Frequency' and 'Percent' respectively), as well as 'Valid percent' and 'Cumulative percent'. Overall, the results show that 60 percent (32 + 28) of respondents had negative or very negative

Attitudes to euthanasia

		Frequency	Percent	Valid Percent	Cumulative percent
Valid	Very positive	4	8.0	8.0	8.0
	Positive	6	12.0	12.0	20.0
	Neutral	10	20.0	20.0	40.0
	Negative	16	32.0	32.0	72.0
	Very negative	14	28.0	28.0	100.0
	Total	50	100.0	100.0	

Figure 4.1

attitudes to euthanasia, 20 per cent were 'neutral' on this matter, and finally, 20 per cent had positive or very positive attitudes to euthanasia (12 + 8 per cent respectively). This offers a general picture of the respondents' feelings on this issue.

Getting crosstabs

What are crosstabs?

Crosstabs are tables containing more than one variable. They may include two (bivariate tables) or more than two variables (multivariate tables).

Example

The views of 100 respondents to gay marriage, expressed in the form of a scale ranging from being strongly against to strongly in favour, were recorded in a survey, including an equal number of men and women. We wish to present the results of this survey in a crosstab so that the views of males and females are displayed separately.

How to get crosstabs

To obtain a crosstab for this example, we proceed as follows:

- Select **Analyze/Descriptive statistics/Crosstabs**.

- Transfer **Gender** to the **Rows** box.

- Transfer **Gay Marriage** to the **Columns** box, and click **OK**.

Gender * 'For/Against Gay Marriage?' Crosstabulation

		For/Against Gay Marriage?					
		Strongly Against	Against	No Opinion	For	Strongly For	Total
Gender	Males	8	9	4	15	14	50
	Females	18	14	4	7	7	50
Total		26	23	8	22	21	100

Figure 4.2

What does this mean?

Figure 4.2 shows the distribution of the respondents' views on gay marriage as well as the proportions of males and females committed to a certain belief regarding this issue. More specifically, the table shows that there are almost twice as many women as men against and strongly against gay marriage. It shows also that there are twice as many men as women for or strongly for gay marriage.

This finding offers a clear and also challenging description of the views of women and men on this issue, and one that will motivate the researcher to take further the analysis, and perhaps look for reasons that generate such a diversity, and also for the significance of these differences.

Mean, mode, median and standard deviation

What is this?

Mean, mode and median are measures of central tendency. The mean describes the average score in the distribution. The median presents the point on a distribution that divides the observations into two equal parts. The mode is the category with the largest number of observations. Standard deviation (SD) is a measure of dispersion, which shows how spread the scores are around the mean.

How to compute them

To obtain all four measures for the age of first-year psychology students we proceed as follows:

- Select **Analyze/Descriptive statistics/Frequencies**.
- Transfer **Age** to the **Variable(s)** box.
- Click on **Statistics** and activate **Mean, Mode, Median** and **Standard deviation**.
- Click on **Continue**, and then click **OK**.

The results are as shown in Figure 4.3.

Statistics		
Age of first year psychology students		
N	Valid	100
	Missing	0
Mean		20.57
Median		20.00
Mode		20
Std. Deviation		1.695

Figure 4.3

What are the results?

The output shows that the average age of first-year psychology students is 20.57 years, the median is 20 years, the mode is 20 years, and the SD is 1.695 years. Whether this SD score is considered small or large is something the analyst has to determine, taking into account factors such as the distribution, the mean score and the nature of the variable.

Which measure of central tendency is most suitable?

For nominal variables	mode.
For ordinal variables	mode and median.
For interval/ratio variables	mode, median and mean.

Standard scores (Z scores)

What is this?

Z scores are 'standardized' numerical scores and are used when scores of different distributions are compared. This standardization converts scores to units expressed in terms of (a) their distance from the mean, measured in standard deviation (SD) units, and (b) whether they are above or below the mean, shown in their +/- sign respectively.

How to compute Z scores

To convert 'age' scores to Z scores we proceed as follows:

- Set raw scores in the variable **Age**.
- Select **Analyze/Descriptive Statistics/Descriptives**.
- Transfer the variable **Age** to the **Variable(s)** box.
- Activate the **Save standardized values as variable**, and then click **OK**.

The Z scores are displayed next to the original scores (see Figure 4.4).

What does this mean?

The Z scores appear next to age scores. Score 12 is converted to -1.6 SDs below the mean. Literally, 12 means 'I am 12 years old'; -1.6 means 'I am younger than most kids in the group'. A girl of the same age may have a Z score of +1.8, meaning she is older than most children in her group. Although both children are 12, this cannot explain their position in

	age	zage	var	var	var	var
1	12	-1.65612				
2	14	-1.19179				
3	15	-.95962				
4	15	-.95962				
5	16	-.72746				
6	17	-.49529				
7	18	-.26312				
8	19	-.03096				
9	20	.20121				
10	21	.43338				
11	22	.66554				
12	23	.89771				
13	24	1.12988				
14	25	1.36205				
15	26	1.59421				
16						

Figure 4.4

their group; their Z score can, for it states that the girl is older and the boy younger than most children in their group. As far as comparison is concerned, Z scores are more informative than raw scores.

Statistics for sub-groups

What is this?

As we saw earlier, tests compute statistics such as mean, media, mode, range and standard deviation for the whole variable. In this section we shall explore the option of computing such tests for parts of a variable, eg for its categories or sub-groups. For instance, instead of, or in addition to, computing the mean and SD of expenses paid for liquor by all (religious and nonreligious) respondents, we may want to compute these measures separately for religious and nonreligious respondents.

How to do it

To obtain the mean and standard deviation of test scores for male and female students who are part of the variable 'Gender' (already in our computer), we proceed as shown below. The statistics for male and female students are shown in Figure 4.5.

- Select **Analyze/Compare means** and click on **Means**.

- Transfer the variable **Scores** to the **Dependent List** box.

- Transfer the variable **Gender** to the **Independent List** box.

- Click **Options**.

- Transfer **Mean** and **Standard Deviation** to the **Cell Statistics** box.

- Click **Continue/OK**.

What does this mean?

This shows that males have a larger mean and a smaller standard deviation than females. This suggests that on average male students did slightly better in the test and were less spread around the mean than were female students. Whether these differences are statistically significant or not is another issue; tests of significance will be discussed in another section. It should be noted that more tests can be included in this procedure, such as median and range.

Report

Student scores

Gender of students	Mean	Std. Deviation
Males	8.46	.897
Females	8.16	.975
Total	8.31	.946

Figure 4.5

Remember!

When we interpret **standard deviation (SD)**, we focus on its size. A small SD score indicates that the scores are clustered closely around the mean, while a large SD score shows that the scores are widely dispersed around the mean. What is considered small or large is something the analyst has to determine, taking into account factors such as the group context, the mean score and the nature of the variable.

CHAPTER 5

Data analysis
Graphic presentations

Many researchers consider graphical presentations early in their analysis, looking for a quick overview of the spread and shape of the distribution. The most common graphs they use are histograms, bar charts, pie charts, scatterplots, boxplots and stem-and-leaf plots, although nowadays the latter seems to be less popular than the others. Graphs come in a variety of formats, as we shall see later in this chapter.

The interpretation of graphs varies according to the nature of the data, the nature of the graph, and the focus of the analyst. Most common points of interpretation are the

- **spread**, ie whether the data is clustered together or wide-spread

- **shape**, ie whether the curve is bell-shaped, J-shaped or U-shaped

- **middle-point**, ie where the centre of the distribution is located

- **outliers**, ie whether there are outliers, how many and how far away they are from the other data.

Graphs are used alone or together with tables and measures of central tendency and dispersion. Graphs will be introduced next.

Important
In graphs, SPSS 15 employs commands that are slightly different from those used in versions 10–14. Hence, where required, commands will be presented separately for each version. Where differences relate to the first step only, in most cases we shall present the instructions as follows:

Step 1   **Vrs 10–14**   Select **Graphs/Bar/Simple** etc.
Step 1   **Vrs 15**   Select **Graphs/Legacy dialogs/** etc.
Step 2   **Vrs 10–15**   Activate **Summaries for groups of cases** etc.

Simply, you begin with 'step 1' of your SPSS version and then go
straight to 'step 2', ignoring the other option for 'step 1'.

Histograms

What is this?

Histograms are graphs used to display frequencies of values in a distribution of continuous data. They contain one variable and are useful
when a quick overview of the spread and shape of the distribution is
required, including asymmetries and outliers.

Example

The age of 100 first-year psychology students was recorded and found
to be between 18 and 24. We wish to obtain a quick overview of the
distribution of age in a graphical form.

How to do it

To display the results in a histogram we follow the steps listed below:

Using SPSS 10–14	Using SPSS 15
Go to **Graphs/Histogram**	Go to **Graphs/Legacy dialogs/Histograms**
Transfer **Age** to the **Variable** box	Transfer **Age** to the **Variable** box.
Check **Display normal curve**, and click **OK**	Check **Display normal curve**, and click **OK**

Following this, the histogram appears in the Viewer as shown in
Figure 5.1.

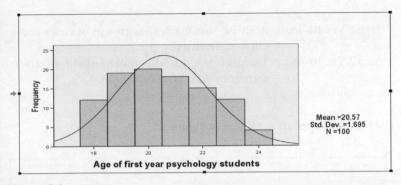

Figure 5.1

What does this mean?

This histogram shows that the age distribution is slightly skewed, with the majority of the students being between 19 and 21 years of age. The extra information on mean, standard deviation and sample size (N) is useful and adds value to the properties of the graph.

Note that Version 15 offers more options for obtaining histograms, but the one offered above is simple, direct and quick, and after all, produces the outcomes we need.

Simple bar charts

What is this?

Bar charts are graphs suitable for nominal and ordinal data. Note that the bars are set apart, ie they are not joined together, as in histograms. Simple bar charts display the distribution of one variable only.

How to get bar charts

To obtain a simple bar chart describing the attitudes to euthanasia, ranging from very positive to very negative, we proceed as follows:

Step 1 **Vrs 10–14**	Select **Graphs/Bar/Simple**.
Step 1 **Vrs 15**	Select **Graphs/Legacy dialogs/Bar/Simple**.

| Step 2 **Vrs 10–15** | Activate **Summaries for groups of cases** and click on **Define**. |
| Step 3 **Vrs 10–15** | Transfer the variable **Euthanasia** to the **Category Axis** box, and click **OK**. |

The bar chart appears as shown in Figure 5.2.

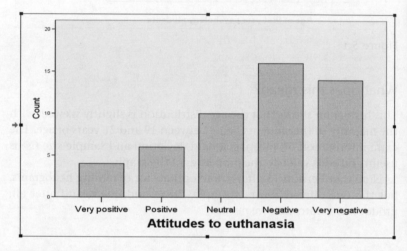

Figure 5.2

What does this mean?

The bar chart shows that the distribution is skewed and that there are many more respondents against than in favour of euthanasia. A sizable group of respondents do not seem to have a firm view on this matter.

Get more
Ask the Chart editor for extras. For instance, you can display labels on the bars containing their size, in 'count' or 'percentage'.

Clustered bar charts

What is this?

Clustered bar charts describe two variables with their values displayed next to each other. These charts not only offer information about the overall shape of the distribution, but allow also easy comparisons between the variables.

How to get bar charts

To obtain a clustered bar chart for the variables Gender and Euthanasia considered in the previous section, we proceed as follows:

Step 1 **Vrs 10–14**	Select **Graphs/Bar/Clustered**.	
Step 1 **Vrs 15**	Select **Graphs/Legacy dialogs/Bar/Clustered**.	
Step 2 **Vrs 10–15**	Activate **Summaries for groups of cases** and click on **Define**.	
Step 3 **Vrs 10–15**	Activate **N of Cases** (if it is not already activated).	
Step 4 **Vrs 10–15**	Transfer **Attitudes** to the **Category Axis** box.	
Step 5 **Vrs 10–15**	Transfer **Gender** to the **Define clusters by** box and click **OK**.	

The result of the computations are presented in the bar chart in Figure 5.3.

What does this chart mean?

Briefly, this shows that the distribution is skewed, for men more than for women, and that more men than women express negative and very negative attitudes to euthanasia. This is particularly so with regard to very negative attitudes to euthanasia.

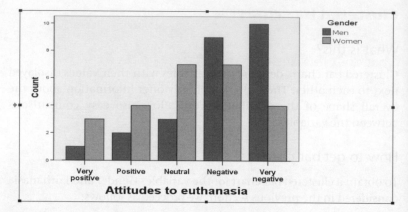

Figure 5.3

Stacked bar charts

What is this?

Stacked bar charts are the same as and serve the same purpose as clustered bar charts; they only differ in the way the bars are displayed.

How to obtain stacked bar charts

To obtain a stacked bar chart for the variables Euthanasia and Gender addressed in the previous section, we proceed as follows:

Step 1 **Vrs 10–14**	Select **Graphs/Bar/Stacked**.
Step 1 **Vrs 15**	Select **Graphs/Legacy dialogs/Bar/Stacked**.
Step 2 **Vrs 10–15**	Activate **Summaries for groups of cases** and click **Define**.
Step 3 **Vrs 10–15**	Activate **N of Cases** (if it is not already activated).
Step 4 **Vrs 10–15**	Transfer **Attitudes** to the **Category Axis** box.
Step 5 **Vrs 10–15**	Transfer **Gender** to the **Define clusters by** box and click **OK**.

The results of the computations are presented in the bar chart in Figure 5.4.

What does this mean?

The interpretation is the same as for clustered bar charts.

By the way
You can change the position of the bars of any bar chart from vertical to horizontal if, while in the Viewer, you click on the chart to activate the Chart editor, click on Option/Transpose chart, make your choice and then click on File/Close.

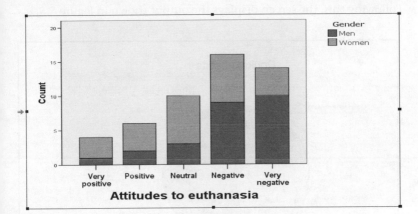

Figure 5.4

Pie charts

What is this?

Pie charts are graphs that are used to display frequency counts in the distribution of one variable. The size of the slice reflects the size of the corresponding category.

How to get a pie chart

To obtain a pie chart to display the drinking habits of the members of a club, ranging from 'compulsive drinking' through 'social drinking' to 'non drinking', we proceed as follows:

Step 1 **Vrs 10–14**	Select **Graphs/Pie**.	
Step 1 **Vrs 15**	Select **Graphs/Legacy dialogs/Pie**.	
Step 2 **Vrs 10–15**	Activate **Summaries for groups of cases** and click on **Define**.	
Step 3 **Vrs 10–15**	Activate **N of cases**.	
Step 4 **Vrs 10–15**	Transfer the variable **Drinking** to **Define slices by** box, and click **OK**.	

Following this, the screen displays the output shown in Figure 5.5.

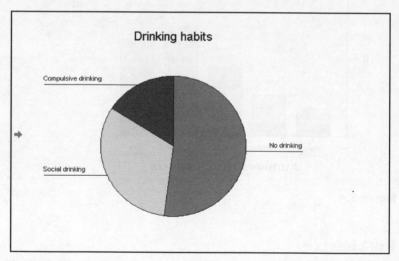

Figure 5.5

What does this mean?

This shows that the largest group of the respondents are non drinkers, followed by 'Social Drinkers', and then by 'Compulsive Drinkers'.

Add 'lift out'

'Lift out' is the highlighting of one or more slices of pie chart by lifting them out of the pie context, as shown in Figure 5.6.

To lift out one (or more) slice(s), you proceed as follows:

- While in the Viewer, double-click on the **Pie Chart** to activate the **Chart editor**.

- Click on the **Pie** to activate it (a circle appears around it).

- Click on the **slice** you wish to accentuate.

- Click on **Elements/Explode slice** (or click on the **Lift out** button).

- Click on **File/Close**.

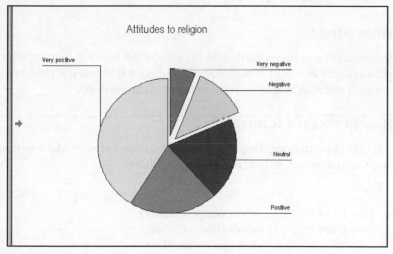

Figure 5.6

Add percentages

You can, finally, insert in each slice the corresponding size (count or percentage). To insert percentages, you proceed as follows:

- Double-click on the pie to activate the **Chart editor**.

- Click **Elements/Show data labels**.

- Highlight **Count** in the **Displayed** box, and click ⊠ to shift Count to the **Not displayed** box.

- Highlight **Percent** in the **Not displayed** box and click the upward arrow to shift Percent to the **Displayed** box.

- Click **Apply/Close**, and then **File/Close**.

Following this, the size of each slice will be given in small labels in percentages. If you prefer counts, proceed as above but skip steps 3 and 4. This is so because 'counts' is set as default in this procedure.

Simple scattergrams

What is this?

Scattergrams are charts that display the association between two variables with numerical values. They provide information about the presence, strength and direction of correlation between the variables.

How to obtain a scattergram

To obtain a scattergram displaying the association between Math scores and Social Research scores, we proceed as follows:

Step 1 **Vrs 10–14**	Select **Graphs/Scatter**.
Step 1 **Vrs 15**	Select **Graphs/Legacy dialogs/Scatter/Dot**.
Step 2 **Vrs 10–15**	Click **Simple** and then **Define**.
Step 3 **Vrs 10–15**	Transfer **SR scores** to **Y-Axis** box and **Math scores** to X-Axis box.
Step 4 **Vrs 10–15**	Click **OK**.

Following this, the Viewer displays the diagram shown in Figure 5.7.

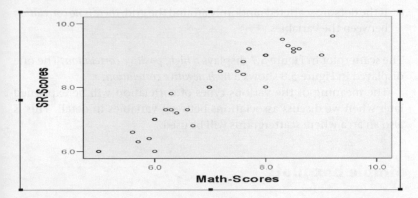

Figure 5.7

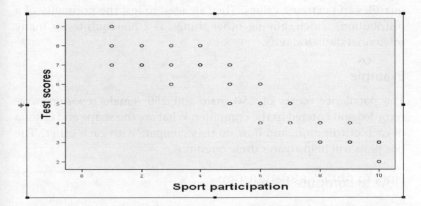

Figure 5.8

What does this mean?

- If the dots cluster around a straight line, *there is a correlation*.

- If they cluster close to the line, the *correlation is strong*; if they are further away from the line, the *correlation is weak*.

- If the dots follow a line running from the top-left corner to the bottom-right corner of the grid, *the correlation is negative*; and if the dots follow a line running from the bottom-left corner to the top-right corner, *the correlation is positive*.

■ If the dots are scattered randomly around the grid, *there is no correlation* between the variables.

The scatterplot in Figure 5.7 displays a *high, positive correlation*. The one displayed in Figure 5.8 shows a *high negative correlation*.

The meaning of the various types of correlation will be explained later when we discuss associations between variables in detail. This is also an area where scattergrams will be used.

Simple box plots

What is this?

Box plots are graphs displaying summary statistics such as median, quartiles and extreme values. They are used to test the normality of a distribution, which, among other things, is a prerequisite for many inferential statistical tests.

Example

The popularity scores of 250 male and 250 female reporters were recorded and entered in the computer. What are the shape and criteria of each distribution, and how do they compare with each other? The box plots will help answer these questions.

How to compute them

To compute simple box plots you proceed as follows.

Step 1 **Vrs 10–14**	Select **Graphs/Boxplots** and click **Simple**.
Step 1 **Vrs 15**	Select **Graphs/Legacy dialogs/Boxplots** and click **Simple**.
Step 2 **Vrs 10–15**	Activate **Summaries of separate variables** and then **Define**.
Step 3 **Vrs 10–15**	Transfer variables **Males** and **Females** to **Boxes represent** box.
Step 4 **Vrs 10–15**	Click **OK**.

The Output in the Viewer displays the box plot shown in Figure 5.9.

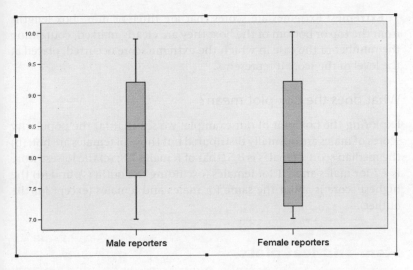

Figure 5.9

Interpretation: the nature of box plots

The box plot contains five elements: a shaded box, a heavy line within it, two lines extending from the box and joined with other lines that are parallel to the box (usually referred to as 'whiskers'), outliers and extremes.

Shaded box: The shaded box is located in the middle of the distribution, covering the interquartile range, and contains 50 per cent of the values. The top side of the box is the 75th percentile, and the bottom side of the box is the 25th percentile.

Heavy line: The heavy line inside the box represents the median of the distribution. If this line is in the centre of the box, the distribution is likely to be normal; if it is close to the top of the box, it is likely to be negatively skewed, and if it is closer to the bottom edge of the box, it is likely to be positively skewed.

Whiskers: The lines that extend from the box are the whiskers, and indicate the highest and the lowest values, excluding outliers. This means that the outliers are not counted when the position of the whiskers is computed.

Outliers: Outliers are scores that are one and a half to three box lengths from the top or bottom edges of the box, and are marked by a circle and a number.

Extremes: Extremes are scores that are three or more box lengths from the top or bottom of the box; they are clearly marked, containing the number of the case in which the extreme score occurred, placed at the level of the score it represents.

What does the box plot mean?

Exploring the box plot of our example, we see that (a) the popularity scores of males are normally distributed but those of females are not; (b) the median score of males is 8.5, that of females 7.8; (c) the lowest score is 7.7 for males and 7.1 for females (excluding the outliers); and (d) the highest score is about the same for males and females (except for the outlier).

Stem-and-leaf plots

What is this?

Stem-and-leaf plots are graphs displaying the frequency of interval data in digits. Stem-and-leaf plots contain three columns. At the centre is the 'Stem'; it contains the scores. The left column contains the frequency scores, and the right column (the 'Leaf'), displays visually the frequencies of each score using zeroes. This plot is not as popular as other graphs, but useful nevertheless, especially for less demanding computer systems

How to get plots

To obtain a stem-and-leaf plot we proceed as follows (for all versions).

- Go to **Analyze/Descriptive Statistics** and click on **Explore**.
- Transfer the numeric variable to the **Dependent List** box.
- Click on **Plots** and activate **Stem-and-Leaf Plot**.
- Click **Continue** and then **OK**.

The output displayed in the Viewer in shown in Figure 5.10.

```
        VAR00001 Stem-and-Leaf Plot

     Frequency      Stem &  Leaf

        2.00  Extremes      (=<1.0)
        5.00         2 .  00000
        6.00         3 .  000000
       10.00         4 .  0000000000
       16.00         5 .  0000000000000000
        9.00         6 .  000000000
        6.00         7 .  000000
        4.00         8 .  0000
        2.00  Extremes      (>=9.0)

     Stem width:           1
     Each leaf:       1 case(s)
```

Figure 5.10

What does this mean?

Like histograms, stem-and-leaf plots focus primarily on the shape of the distribution. The plot above shows that the scores are normally distributed around score 5, which displays the largest number of observations.

Transform charts

What is this?

Already constructed charts can be converted to other formats, eg pie charts to bar charts, line charts or area charts, with a simple mouse click – or two! This option is employed for instance when searching for a more appropriate explanation of the results, or when opting for a multiple presentation. For instance, sometimes it is easier to compare the categories when they are expressed in bars rather than in pie slices.

Here is how you convert a pie chart to a bar chart. While in the Viewer:

Using SPSS 14:

- Double-click on the **Pie chart** to activate the **Chart editor**.
- Click again on the **Pie chart** and select **Transform**.

- Click **Simple bar**.

- Click **Close** to close the **Properties** window, and then on **File/Close**.

  When using SPSS 15, you proceed as follows:

- Double-click on the **Pie chart** to activate the **Chart editor**.

- Click once on the **Pie chart**, and then choose **Edit/Properties**.

- Open the **Elements Type** box, click **Bar**, click **Apply**.

- Click **Close** to close the **Properties** window, and then choose **File/Close**.

Following this, the pie chart shown in Figure 5.11 is transformed to the bar chart, placed next to it.

The same procedure is followed when transforming other types of charts. You only need to make your choice when in the 'Elements Type' box.

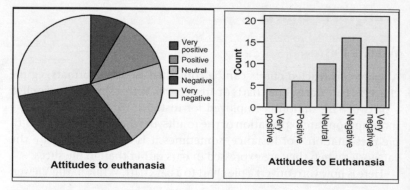

Figure 5.11

CHAPTER 6

Tests of significance
Nonparametric tests

The main aim of research is to study aspects of social life, of society or – better – of the population. However, researchers usually study samples of the population. The question now is: Do sample results count for the population? Can their results be applied to the population? Significance tests can assist with these questions. There are two types of significance tests, parametric and nonparametric tests. *Parametric tests* assume, among other things, that the population from which samples have been taken is normally distributed, and compare means. *Non-parametric* tests do not assume normality of the population, and compare frequencies. The most popular tests of significance are shown in Table 6.1.

How do we choose the right test? The choice is determined by (a) the level of measurement; (b) the number of samples; (c) the nature of samples, ie being dependent or independent; and (d) whether the population is assumed to be normally distributed or not. In this chapter we shall introduce significance and nonparametric tests.

A note on statistical significance

Statistical significance is the probability that a test result has occurred by chance or error. In practice, this probability is expressed in levels (significance levels, or α levels) and researchers testing the significance of their results work within these levels. The most popular levels are .05 and .01. Level .05 means that the probability that a test result has occurred by chance or error is 5 per cent, or 5 in 100. Level .01 assumes that this probability is 1 per cent or 1 in 100.

Basically, to assess the significance of test outcomes, researchers (a) conduct a test and compute the **p-value**, ie the significance of the test result; (b) choose a significance level, say .05; and then (c) interpret the

Table 6.1

	Nonparametric tests		Parametric tests
Number and type of samples	Nominal level	Ordinal level	Interval/ratio level
One	χ^2-test (Goodness-of-fit test)	Kolmogorov-Smirnov test	t-test
Two independent	χ^2-test of independence Fisher's exact test z-test for proportions	Mann-Whitney U-test Wald-Wolfowitz runs test	t-test
Two dependent	McNemar test	Sign test Wilcoxon test	t-test
More than two independent	χ^2-test	Kruskal-Wallis H-test	ANOVA
More than two dependent	Cochran Q-test	Friedman test	ANOVA

From: S. Sarantakos (2005) *Social Research,* Melbourne: Macmillan

results by comparing the p-value with the significance level. If the p-value is within the region of the significance level, here .05, the results are said to be significant at the .05 level; otherwise they are not significant. But what are the boundaries of the region? What is the top value of the significance level? There are two ways of interpreting the region, both equally legitimate and popular. With regard to .05 level, and with respect to an association test the options are as follows:

Option A	**p < .05**	The test result is significant if the p-value is **below .05**
Option B	**p ≤ .05**	The test result is significant if the p-value is **.05 or less**

The critical point here is that, for Option A, .05 does not belong to the region of the significance level .05; this level includes all values below .05 but not .05. Hence a p-value of .05 is not significant. However, for

Table 6.2

If the p value is	The associations, differences etc. are	Sign level	Symbol
> 0.05	Not significant	–	ns
0.01 – 0.05	Significant	.05	*
0.001 – 0.01	Very significant	.01	**
< 0.001	Extremely significant	.001	***

Option B, .05 does belong to the region of .05, hence a p-value of .05 is significant. More information about the levels of significance, and their ranks, levels and symbols is shown in Table 6.2.

This table makes significance testing rather simple; it only involves fitting the p value into the regions of the significance levels. We shall see later that SPSS makes this task even easier, for it takes over this task and using the asterisks above detects and defines significance for us.

Chi-square test: goodness-of-fit test

What is this?

This is a nonparametric test of significance, and is used to compare one sample with a nominal variable, and with frequency data. This test compares the observed frequencies with the expected frequencies.

Expected differences are constructed on the basis of two assumptions, namely (a) that all groups are equal, ie that the variable in question is distributed equally among the groups of the study; or (b) that the groups are unequal, and the variable in question is not distributed equally among the groups of the study. Whether to use the one assumption or the other depends on the nature of the question. One point to consider is that the expected values in each cell need to be larger than 5. The computer will display how many cells contain less than 5 expected values.

Example

A study of 100 men found that 52 are non drinkers, 32 social drinkers and 16 compulsive drinkers. Are these groups significantly different?

If the groups are assumed to be equal, the expected frequencies would be 33.3 for each group, ie one third of men are expected to be compulsive drinkers, one third social drinkers and one third non-drinkers. If there is evidence to suggest that the groups are known to be unequal, ie 50 per cent non-drinkers, 30 per cent social drinkers and 20 per cent compulsive drinkers, then the expected frequencies will follow this pattern. Briefly, in the goodness-of-fit test, and when estimating the significance level, the expectations determine the standards used to compare the various groups of the sample. There is a test for each case, namely for equal categories and for unequal categories, and we shall explore both next.

Computation: equal categories

Considering the sample above where the three different groups of respondents were assumed to be equal, the computation proceeds as follows:

- Select **Analyze/Non-parametric tests** and click on **Chi-square**.

- Transfer **Drinking** to the **Test variable list** box.

- Activate **All categories equal**.

- Click on **Options** and activate **Descriptive**.

- Click on **Continue/OK**.

The computation results are displayed in the Viewer as shown in Figure 6.1. The first table in the figure contains a frequency table of the drinking habits of the respondents. The expected frequencies are shown to be equal (33.3 each). The other table shows the test statistics.

What are we looking for?

We focus on...	We ask...	What does this mean?
P-value – (Asymp. Sig.)	Is the p-value below the significance level?	If yes, the differences are significant, otherwise they are not significant.

Drinking habits

	Observed N	Expected N	Residual
Non-drinkers	52	33.3	18.7
Social drinkers	32	33.3	-1.3
Compulsive drinkers	16	33.3	-17.3
Total	100		

Test Statistics

	Drinking habits
Chi-Square[a]	19.520
df	2
Asymp. Sig.	.000

a. 0 cells (.0%) have expected frequencies less than 5. The minimum expected cell frequency is 33.3

Figure 6.1

What does this mean?

Important for the comparison of the three groups is the p-value, which is .000. As we already know, if this value is below the significance level, the differences between the groups are 'extremely significant'. In simple terms this means that the three groups are not equal, but different from each other. The numerical differences are also significant.

Computation: unequal categories

If we have reasons to believe that the expected frequencies are not equal but different, eg as suggested above, one half (50 per cent) non-drinkers, 30 per cent drink socially and 20 per cent drink compulsively, the computation of chi-square will proceed as follows:

- Select **Analyze/Non-parametric tests**.
- Click on **Chi-square**, and transfer **Drinking** to **Test variable list** box.
- Activate **Values**, then enter **50** and click on **Add**.
- Enter **30** and click on **Add**; then enter **20** and click on **Add**.
- Click on **Options** and activate **Descriptive**.
- Click on **Continue/OK**.

Following this, the Viewer displays the output shown in Figure 6.2.

Drinking habits

	Observed N	Expected N	Residual
Non-drinkers	52	50.0	2.0
Social drinkers	32	30.0	2.0
Compulsive drinkers	16	20.0	-4.0
Total	100		

Test Statistics

	Drinking habits
Chi-Square[a]	1.013
df	2
Asymp. Sig.	.603

a. 0 cells (.0%) have expected frequencies less than 5. The minimum expected cell frequency is 20.0.

Figure 6.2

What are we looking for?

We focus on...	We ask...	What does this mean?
P-value – (Asymp. Sig.)	Is the p-value below the significance level?	If yes, the differences are significant, otherwise they are not significant.

What does this mean?

Focusing on the p-value ('Asymp. Sig.'), we find that the p-value is .603. We already know that when the p-value is above .05, the differences are not significant. Given that our value is far above .05 (.603 > .05), we can argue that the three groups are not significantly different. Hence we can say that the observed frequencies are as unequal as the expected frequencies. Simply, the comparison of the groups reveals that they are not significantly different.

Chi-square test for independence

What is this?

This is a nonparametric test for nominal level data, that is used to test whether the groups in question are independent, or in other words to test whether groups vary significantly with regard to a particular criterion.

Example

A survey of men and women produced the following findings regarding their drinking habits (Table 6.3).

Table 6.3

Gender	No drinking	Social drinking	Compulsive drinking	Total
Males	26	18	06	50
Females	28	18	04	50

The question here is whether men and women drink in equal numbers; or whether Gender and Drinking are independent. The chi-square test for independence will guide our procedure.

How to compute it

To conduct this test, we first enter the table data in the computer as tabular data (see Chapter 2). We then proceed as follows:

- Select **Analyze/Descriptive Statistics/Crosstabs**.

- Transfer **Gender** to **Row(s)** box, and **Drinking** to **Column(s)** box.

- Click on **Statistics** and activate **Chi-square**.

- Click on **Continue/OK**.

The results are shown Figure 6.3. The table in the figure shows the chi-square value, the degrees of freedom (df) and the p-value in the 'Asymp. Sign' column.

Chi-Square Tests

	Value	df	Asymp. Sign (2-sided)
Pearson Chi-Square	.474(a)	2	.789
Likelihood ratio	.477	2	788
Linear-by-linear Association	.355	1	551
N of Valid Cases	100		

a 0 cells (.0%) have expected count less than 5. The minimum expected count is 5.00.

Figure 6.3

What are we looking for?

We focus on...	We ask...	What does this mean?
P-value – (Asymp. Sig.)	Is the p-value below the significance level?	If yes, the differences are significant, otherwise they are not significant.

As previously, we focus on the p-value, which is .789. This suggests that the differences in drinking between males and females are not significant, and hence Gender and Drinking are independent, ie males and females do not differ significantly in their drinking habits.

McNemar test

What is this?

This is a nonparametric test for nominal data. It is suitable for two related samples, eg before–after design, where it is usually examined whether an experimental intervention produced any changes in the responses. In other words, it aims to establish whether the data vary significantly with regard to a particular criterion.

Example

In an interview concerning marital expectations 114 young men were asked to state whether they expected their future wife to be good looking. After marriage they were asked again whether their wife was in fact as good looking as they expected her to be. The results are shown in Table 6.4. Are there significant differences between what men expected their future wife to be and how they perceived her to be when married?

Table 6.4 Marital expectations

Was she to be good looking?	Was she good looking?	
	Yes (1)	No (2)
Yes (1)	18	50
No (2)	22	24

How to compute it

To answer the question we conduct McNemar's test proceeding as follows:

- Select **Analyze/Nonparametric tests** and click on **2 Related Samples**.

- Highlight the two variables (before–after) consecutively.

- Transfer the variables to **Test Pair(s) List** box.

- Activate **McNemar** and click **OK**.

Upon completion of these steps the output is displayed in the Viewer. The information we are interested in is displayed in the 'Test Statistics' table (see Figure 6.4 overleaf).

Test Statistics[b]

	Was she to be good looking & Was she good looking
N	114
Chi-Square[a]	10.125
Asymp. Sig.	.001

a. Continuity Corrected

b. McNemar Test

Figure 6.4

What are we looking for?

We focus on...	We ask...	What does this mean?
P-value – (Asymp. Sig.)	Is the p-value below the significance level?	If yes, the differences are significant, otherwise they are not significant.

As always, the decisive figure is the p-value. We know now that a value of below .05 means statistical significance. Also, significant differences mean that the results of the before–after test are significantly different and not produced by error or chance.

What do the results mean?

The p-level (Asymp. Sig.) is .001, which indicates that the differences are very significant. Hence, we conclude that the differences in men's perception of their wife's physical appearance before and after marriage are significant. Substantively speaking, this means that the expectations men have before marriage regarding the physical appearance of their wife are significantly different from the perception they have after marriage.

The Wilcoxon signed-ranks test

What is this?

This is a nonparametric test suitable for ordinal level variables and two related samples. It is used to compare two distributions and to assess whether there is a significant difference between them. This uses the z-test to compute the differences.

Example

Two memory tests were conducted, one before and one after consuming a set amount of alcohol. Is there a significant difference between the test ranks of the before–after memory tests?

How to compute it

To conduct Wilcoxon's test we proceed as follows:

- Select **Analyze/Nonparametric tests**.

- Click on **2 Related Samples**.

- Transfer the two variables (before–after) to the **Test Pair(s) List** box.

- Activate **Wilcoxon** and click **OK**.

Following this, the Viewer displays a number of tables; the 'Test Statistics' table contains the most relevant information (see Figure 6.5).

Test Statistics[b]

	Memory-test 2 – Memory-test 1
Z	-3.078[a]
Asymp. Sig (2tailed)	.002

a. Based on positive ranks

b. Wilcoxon Signed Ranks Test

Figure 6.5

What are we looking for?

We focus on...	We ask...	What does this mean?
P-value – (Asymp. Sig.)	Is the p-value below the significance level?	If yes, the differences are significant, otherwise they are not significant.

What does this mean?

The focus of our analysis is on the 'Test Statistics' table and on the p-value, which is .002. This suggests a significance at the .01 level; hence we can argue that the two sets of test ranks differ 'very significantly'.

Mann-Whitney U test

What is this?

This is a nonparametric test for unrelated samples and for ordinal variables. It is used to compare two distributions and assess whether there is a significant difference between them.

Example

The level of satisfaction of children of ethnic couples and non-ethnic couples was measured (rank scores). Are there any significant differences between the two groups of children? Are ethnic children more or less satisfied than non-ethnic children?

How to compute it

To conduct the Mann-Whitney U test we proceed as follows:

- Select **Analyze/Nonparametric Tests/2 Independent Samples**.
- Transfer **Couples** to the **Grouping Variable** box.
- Select **Define Groups**.

- Enter **1** in Group 1 box and **2** in **Group 2** box, for ethnic and non-ethnic children respectively.

- Click on **Continue**.

- Activate **Mann-Whitney U** and click **OK**.

Of the tables displayed on the screen, the 'Test Statistics' table contains the most relevant information (see Figure 6.6).

Test Statistics[b]

	Satisfaction
Mann-Whitney U	31.673
Z	-3.159
Asymp. Sig.(2-tailed)	.008
Exact Sig. [2*(1-tailed Sig.)]	.006[a]

a. Not corrected for ties

b. Grouping Variable: Couples

Figure 6.6

What do the results mean?

Our focus is on the Mann-Whitney U value (31.673), and more so on its p-value, which is .008, and which suggests that the differences are 'very significant' (at the .01 level). This indicates that the differences in the level of satisfaction of children of ethnic couples and non-ethnic couples – as identified in the study – are statistically significant.

CHAPTER 7

Tests of significance
Parametric tests

In this chapter we explore the second way of testing significance, using parametric tests. There are two such tests: the t-test and the ANOVA test, both comparing means and each being available in a variety of forms as required by the nature and number of samples compared, and the nature of the variables. Table 7.1 describes the various forms of the parametric tests and the areas in which they are employed.

Table 7.1 Which parametric test do I use and when?

Number and type of samples	Interval/ratio level
One sample	t-test
Two unrelated samples	t-test
Two related samples	t-test
More than two unrelated samples	ANOVA
More than two related samples	ANOVA

Simply, this table shows which tests are used and when. For instance, when two related samples are compared and the variables are interval/ratio, a t-test is appropriate, and when three unrelated samples with interval/ratio variables are compared, the ANOVA test should be employed. In summary, parametric tests compare means and are used (a) when the variables are measured at the interval/ratio level; and (b) when the population is considered to be distributed normally.

> **Remember!**
> **Related samples:** these samples contain either the same subjects tested at two different times, or matched subjects (also called *matched* or *dependent* samples). **Unrelated samples:** these contain different and not matched subjects (also called *independent* samples).

T-test for one sample

What is this?

This is a test used to compare the mean of the sample with a set value (a constant). It is employed to test whether there are significant differences between the two.

Example

Do four-cylinder cars consume more than 10 litres per 100 km (10 is the constant). Figures for 20 four-cylinder cars were obtained and entered in the computer. We employ the t-test to address this issue.

How to compute it

To compute the t value we proceed as follows:

- Select **Analyze/Compare means/One-sample T-Test.**
- Transfer **Petrol** to **Test variable(s)** box.
- Type **10** in **Test value** box.
- Click on **Options** and set **Confidence interval** to **95%.**
- Activate **Exclude cases analysis by analysis** (in 'Missing values' sector).
- Click on **Continue/OK.**

The Viewer displays the table shown in Figure 7.1.

One-Sample Test

	Test Value = 10					
					95% Confidence Interval of the Difference	
	t	df	Sig. (2-tailed)	Mean Difference	Lower	Upper
Petrol consumption	4.042	19	.001	2.25	1.08	3.42

Figure 7.1

What does this mean?

The point that offers the decisive answer to our question is the p-value, here shown under 'Sig. (2-tailed)'; its value is .001, and it is 'very significant'. This is sufficient for us to argue that, on average, petrol consumption of four-cylinder cars per 100 kilometres is not 10 litres.

T-test for unrelated (independent) samples

What is this?

This test is used to compare the means of two unrelated samples on one variable, and tests whether there are significant differences between them.

Example

The time spent by 20 males and 20 females in sport activities during a week was recorded. Is there a significant difference between males and females on this activity? To answer this question, the t-test for independent samples will be employed.

How to compute it

To compute the t value we proceed as follows:

- Select **Analyze/Compare means/Independent-samples T-Test**.

- Transfer **Sport** to **Test variable(s)** box.

- Transfer **Sex** to **Grouping variable** box.

- Click **Define Groups**.

- Enter **1** (for Males) in the top box and **2** (for Females) in the other.

- Click **Continue** and then on **Options**.

- Set **Confidence interval** to **95%**.

- Click **Continue** and then **OK**.

The computer output is displayed in the Viewer and the table that contains the essential information for our analysis is shown in Figure 7.2.

What are we looking for?

We focus on...	We ask...	What does this mean?
P-value of Levene's Test	Is the p-value significant?	If yes, we take the option 'unequal variances'; otherwise we take the option 'equal variances'
Sig. (2-tailed)	Is the p-value significant?	If yes, the differences are significant; otherwise they are not significant

1 The output in the **Independent Samples Test** table shows two sets of values: one for equal variances and one for unequal variances. Which one are we supposed to use? The answer to this is given by 'Levene's Test of Equality of Variances' and is briefly described in the summary table above. Hence, the first step in our analysis is to assess the results of Levene's test.

2 The other point we need to address is the p-value in the column 't-test for equality of means' which is listed under '2 Sig. (2-tailed)', and

especially that which was determined by the Levene's test (for equal or unequal variables). The p-value is interpreted as we did previously.

What do the results mean?

1 First we focus on Levene's test, which is .716. Given that this is above .05, ie not significant, we take the option of equal variances.

2 The second important point is the p-value given in the column 'Sig. (2-tailed)'. Of the two values given in this column, we take the one determined by Levene's test, namely the one for equal variances, which is .429. Since the p-valuel is larger than .05 we conclude that the means of the groups of males and females are not significantly different. Substantively speaking, men's sport involvement is not different from that of women.

Independent Samples Test

		Levene's Test for Equality of Variances		t-test for Equality of Means					95% Confidence Interval of the Difference	
		F	Sig.	t	df	Sig. (2-tailed)	Mean Difference	Std. Error Difference	Lower	Upper
Sport involvement	Equal variances assumed	.135	.716	.799	38	.429	.70	.88	-1.07	2.47
	Equal variances not assumed			.799	37.79	.429	.70	.88	-1.07	2.47

Figure 7.2

Note

If the p-value is the same for equal and unequal variances, Levene's test has no purpose, for whatever its answer, the p-value we will use will be the same anyway. In such cases, skipping Levene's test and going straight to t is a quicker option.

T-test for related (dependent) samples

What is this?

This t-test is used to compare means of paired (related) samples, namely samples tested using a before–after measurement, or samples where subjects are matched. The main aim is to test whether the differences between the means of the two samples are statistically significant.

Example

The attitude of 20 students to illegal drug use was measured before and after visiting a drug rehabilitation clinic, and relevant scores were recorded and entered in the computer. We use a t-test to assess the significance of the difference between the two data sets.

How to compute it

To obtain the t value we proceed as follows:

- Select **Analyze/Compare means** and click on **Paired-samples T-Test**.

- Transfer variables to **Paired variable(s)** box and click on **Options**.

- Set **Confidence interval** to 95%, and set **Missing values** as required.

- Click on **Continue** and then **OK**.

The most relevant part of the output (third table) is shown in Figure 7.3.

What are we looking for?

We focus on...	We ask...	What does this mean?
P-value – Sig. (2-tailed)	Is the p-value significant?	If yes, the differences are significant, otherwise they are not significant.

Paired Samples Test

		Paired Differences							
					95% Confidence Interval of the Difference				
		Mean	Std. Deviation	Std. Error Mean	Lower	Upper	t	df	Sig. (2-tailed)
Pair 1	Pretest - Posttest	-1.950	1.701	.380	-2.746	-1.154	-5.128	19	.000

Figure 7.3

In other words, if Sig. is less than .05, the means of the pre-test and post-test scores are taken to be significantly different, and if it is larger than .05 we assume that the means of the pre-test and post-test scores are not significantly different.

What do the results tell us?

Looking at the bottom table under 'Sig. (2-tailed)', we see that the p-value is .000, which indicates that the differences between the pre-test and post-test are 'extremely significant'. Hence, we conclude that the differences between the pre-test and post-test results are significantly different. Taking this a step further we can say that the exposure of the subjects to the rehabilitation centre and to its residents may have had an impact on their attitudes to drug use.

Remember!
One-tailed tests are those in which the region of rejection is on one 'tail' of the sampling distribution, and are *directional*. For instance, when tests show that males are taller than females, and when these differences are found to be significant, we can state that 'males are taller than females'.

Two-tailed tests are those in which the region of rejection falls within both tails of the sampling distribution and are *non-directional*. For instance, in the previous example, we can state that 'the body height of males is different from that of females'. (It does not state who is taller.)

One-way analysis of variance (ANOVA)

What is this?

This is a parametric test employed to compare the means of two or more distributions. It is suitable for variables measured at the interval/ratio level; it is very commonly used, and is similar to t-tests, but it is not restricted to two samples, as t-tests are. ANOVA is also known as the F-test.

Example

A survey including same-age students from Australia, Austria, Greece and the USA was conducted to explore their attitudes toward families. The results were collected and entered in the computer. One of the aims of the study was to ascertain whether the attitudes of the students varied significantly.

How to compute it

To compute a one-way ANOVA test we proceed as follows:

- Select **Analyze/Compare means**.

- Click on **One way ANOVA**.

- Transfer the dependent variable **Familism** to the **Dependent List** box.

- Transfer factor variable **Country** to the Factor box.

- Select **Options/Descriptive**.

- Click **Continue**.

- Click **OK**.

Upon completion of these steps the Viewer displays the output shown in Figure 7.4. This includes the Descriptives table as well as the ANOVA table, also known as the F-Table. The Descriptives table shows the descriptives of the various groups, namely mean, standard deviation, standard error of the mean, confidence intervals, minimum and maximum. The ANOVA table contains the information that is most important for us at this stage at least, and this is the one on which we shall concentrate next.

Descriptives

Familism scores

	N	Mean	Std. Deviation	Std. Error	95% Confidence Interval for Mean		Minimum	Maximum
					Lower Bound	Upper Bound		
Australia	15	2.47	.52	.13	2.18	2.75	2	3
Austria	15	3.00	.65	.17	2.64	3.36	2	4
Greece	15	4.53	.52	.13	4.25	4.82	4	5
USA	15	2.47	.52	.13	2.18	2.75	2	3
Total	60	3.12	1.01	.13	2.86	3.38	2	5

ANOVA

Familism scores

	Sum of Squares	df	Mean Square	F	Sig.
Between Groups	42.983	3	14.328	46.649	.000
Within Groups	17.200	56	.307		
Total	60.183	59			

Figure 7.4

The ANOVA table

The ANOVA table shows that the total variation is partitioned into the *between groups* variation and the *within groups* variation. The former refers to the variation of the group means from the overall mean. The latter refers to the variation of individual scores from their group mean. Last, but not least, the F-Table contains the p-value (Sig.) which often is used as the central focus of the process of interpretation.

What are we looking for?

We focus on...	We ask...	What does this mean?
P-value – (Sig.)	Is the p-value significant?	If yes, the differences are significant, otherwise they are not significant.

What does this mean?

Given that our p-value is .000, we conclude that the differences between the groups are 'extremely significant', and hence at least one group differs significantly from the others.

Post hoc comparisons

What is this?

This test is an extension of ANOVA, and answers a question which ANOVA cannot answer. As noted in the previous section, the results of the ANOVA test tells us whether there are significant differences between the groups, and if there are, it allows the conclusion that at least one of the groups differs from the others. But it can tell us neither how many groups differ nor which are the groups that differ. Post hoc comparisons tell us just that: which groups differ, and whether these differences are significant.

Example

In the family attitudes study reported in the previous section, the ANOVA test reported that at least one of these samples differs from the others. We now want to know which samples differ from the others and which ones do not. Post hoc comparisons will be used to answer this question.

How to compute it

To compute Post hoc comparisons we proceed as follows:

- Select **Analyze/Compare means**, and click on **ANOVA**.
- Transfer **Familism** to **Dependent List** box.
- Transfer **Country** to **Factor** box.
- Click on **Post Hoc** and activate **Tukey**.
- Click on **Continue** and then click **OK**.

The results of this computation are shown in the Viewer. The important information is contained in the table 'Multiple Comparisons' (see Figure 7.5).

What are we looking for?

We are now looking for the country or countries that differ significantly from each other. To identify this – using the quick way – we look at the values displayed in the 'Mean Difference' column, and particularly at those that are marked with an asterisk. Those with an asterisk are the countries that differ significantly.

Before we start checking this we must become acquainted with the logic of the first left-hand side column of the table. This presents comparisons between one country and the other three countries separately. For instance, the first row in the first column compares Australia with the other three countries. The second row compares Austria with the other three countries; and so on.

The result of the comparisons is given in the 'Mean Difference (I–J)' column. For instance, for Australia the result of the comparisons indicates that it has a lower mean than Austria (–.53), lower than Greece (–2.07), and that there is no difference between the means of Australia and USA. Of all three comparisons, the only one that produced a significant difference is that with the asterisk: the difference between Australia and Greece

Multiple Comparisons

Dependent Variable: Familism scores
Tukey HSD

(I) Country of birth	(J) Country of birth	Mean Difference (I-J)	Std. Error	Sig.	95% Confidence Interval	
					Lower Bound	Upper Bound
Australia	Austria	-.53	.20	.052	-1.07	2.52E-03
	Greece	-2.07*	.20	.000	-2.60	-1.53
	USA	.00	.20	1.000	-.54	.54
Austria	Australia	.53	.20	.052	-2.52E-03	1.07
	Greece	-1.53*	.20	.000	-2.07	-1.00
	USA	.53	.20	.052	-2.52E-03	1.07
Greece	Australia	2.07*	.20	.000	1.53	2.60
	Austria	1.53*	.20	.000	1.00	2.07
	USA	2.07*	.20	.000	1.53	2.60
USA	Australia	.00	.20	1.000	-.54	.54
	Austria	-.53	.20	.052	-1.07	2.52E-03
	Greece	-2.07*	.20	.000	-2.60	-1.53

*. The mean difference is significant at the .05 level.

Figure 7.5

is statistically significant. To identify other significant differences we approach the rest of the table in a similar manner.

What does this mean?

Examining the comparisons between each country and the other three we find that Greece is the only country that differs significantly from the others. The differences between the other countries are not significant. This supports the conclusion that the attitudes of the various groups of students to family do not differ significantly, except for Greek students. In this sense, post hoc comparisons refine the results produced by ANOVA and provide more specific and more accurate information about group comparisons than ANOVA does.

CHAPTER 8

Correlation tests
For nominal variables

In this chapter we shall address a number of methods employed to test associations between variables. Such methods assist analysts to answer questions such as whether class status is associated with childlessness, or whether gender is associated with attitudes to monarchy.

More specifically, correlation tests can inform the analyst, for instance, whether an increase in the independent variable is followed by an increase in the dependent variable and vice versa (positive correlation); or whether an increase in the independent variable leads to a decrease in the dependent variable (negative correlation). For example, is it true that the more time students spend studying, the higher their test scores? Or the more time students spend doing sport, the lower their test scores?

There are three different groups of tests of correlation, namely tests for nominal variables, ordinal variables and for interval/ratio variables. The tests employed in each group are listed in Table 8.1.

Table 8.1 Which test do I use and when?

If your variables are	You use the test
Nominal	ϕ (phi) coefficient, Cramer's V or Lambda (λ)
Ordinal	Spearman's rho, Gamma (γ) or Somers' d
Interval/ratio	Pearson's r

Correlation tests produce, among other things, a correlation coefficient and a p value. The former describes some aspects of correlation and the latter the level of significance of the correlation reported in the test. In this chapter we shall introduce correlations as a part of data analysis as well as statistical significances, before we explore correlation tests for nominal variables.

Correlation tests

As we shall see soon, the information offered by the tests varies significantly. Some tests provide information about the presence, strength and direction of an association, while others inform about the presence of an association only. Some offer fine details about the association; others are restricted to general trends. Interval/ratio correlation tests belong to the first group; nominal tests to the latter.

What are correlation tests?

Correlation tests are statistical procedures used to establish whether there is a relationship between variables, ie whether they are interconnected so that when the one changes the other will also change, in some way and to some degree. For instance, we might want to know whether there is an association between religiosity and divorce rates, that is, whether religious couples are more or less likely to divorce than non-religious couples. Likewise, we might be interested in the relationship between use of mobile phone and brain tumours, namely whether people using mobile phones are more likely to develop brain tumours than those not using mobile phones.

Types of correlation tests

There are three major types of correlation tests: tests suitable for data measured at the nominal level, and others for data measured at the ordinal, and interval or ratio level. Table 8.1 shows the correlation tests that correspond to each of these three groups.

Correlations for nominal variables

These correlation tests are employed when data are measured at the nominal level, such as Gender (males–females), Race (black–white), and Religion (Catholic, Protestant, other). Of the correlation tests listed in the table above for this type of tests, phi (ϕ) coefficient, and Cramer's V are chi-square based measures; lambda is a PRE (proportional reduction in error) measure. Due to their nature, nominal level measures of association offer information about the *strength* but *not the direction* of the association, hence there are no negative correlations in this group.

Correlations for ordinal variables

There are two types of measures for data measured at the ordinal level: (a) those based on concordant–discordant comparisons, and (b) those based on correlation. Gamma, Somers' d, Kendall's tau-b (τ_b) and Kendall's tau-c (τ_c) belong to the first group. Spearman's rho belongs to the second group.

Gamma, Somers' d, Kendall's tau-b (τ_b) and Kendall's tau-c (τ_c) are suitable only for crosstabulated frequency distributions and not if data are measured as continuous variables. All but Somers' d are symmetric (nondirectional). These measures examine the association between the variables by comparing concordant and discordant pairs. Concordant pairs are those where the two respondents are ranked the same way in both variables; discordant pairs are those that are ranked differently.

Unlike nominal level correlation tests, ordinal level tests provide information not only about the *strength* of the relationship between the variables in question but also about the *direction* of the association. Coefficients here can be *positive* or *negative*.

Correlations for interval/ratio variables

As noted above, the correlation that is considered to be appropriate for interval/ratio variables is product-moment correlation, or Pearson's r, as it is usually referred to. More specifically, Pearson's correlation is a symmetrical, interval/ratio level test, and deals with pairs of scores, and with magnitudes (not with ranks). It helps to establish whether there is a linear correlation between two variables, and if so, whether this correlation is strong/weak, and positive or negative. In other words Pearson's r informs both about the *strength* and the *direction* of the relationship.

Assessing a correlation output.

How do we analyse the results of correlation tests? The box below shows how to start; the next section illustrates how to proceed further. Note that the part on negative correlation does not apply to nominal variables.

We focus on...	We ask...
1 Coefficient value	Does it indicate a strong, weak, positive or negative correlation?
2 P-value	Is the p-value significant?

As noted above, correlation analysis focuses on the coefficient and on the p-value. Let us explain this in more detail, including their meaning.

The coefficient: In general, a correlation coefficient indicates the *presence*, *direction* (positive or negative), and *strength* of the relationship (low, high, etc. correlation). The coefficient ranges from –1 (perfect negative correlation) to +1 (perfect positive correlation). A zero correlation indicates no association between the variables. Statistics texts describe the grading of the strength of the relationship as shown in Table 8.2.

Table 8.2

Correlation coefficient	Strength of relationship
<.01	No correlation
.01 – .20	Very low; almost negligible
.21 – .40	Low; definite but small
.41 – .70	Moderate; substantial
.71 – .90	High; marked
.91 – 1.00	Very high and dependable

The direction of correlation: Correlation can be positive or negative; in the former the coefficient is marked by a '+' and in the latter by a '–'. In a positive correlation an increase in the one variable is associated with an increase in the other (the higher the one variable the higher the other). In a negative correlation, an increase in the one variable is associated with a decrease in the other (the higher the one variable the lower the other).

Statistical significance: As in other tests, a correlation is significant if the p-value is less than the chosen significance level, eg less than .05. Otherwise, it is not significant (even if the r value is high). Being significant means that the findings were not produced by error or chance. (Note that there is another way of assessing statistical significance, namely by considering a correlation to be significant if the p-value is exactly the significance level or less, eg .05 or less.)

It is worth noting that the availability of the three attributes of correlation coefficient varies with the type of correlation, ie whether it is a nominal, ordinal or interval/ratio correlation. Pay attention to this point when the various types of correlation are introduced.

In the following, we shall explore some of the correlation tests introduced above, starting with tests for nominal variables. Only the most common tests will be considered.

Caution!
Don't confuse association with causation. Association tests investigate relations between variables and not causation; they study whether the variables are associated and not whether the one can cause the other.

Phi (ϕ) and Cramer's V

What is this?

Phi and Cramer's V test the association between variables, of which at least one is nominal, ie it is measured as a true dichotomy, such as gender (Male–Female). Often, both tests produce the same coefficient values; this is obvious since they both are chi-square based measures.

This is so for 2 x 2 tables. For larger tables, Phi values can go beyond 1, making conclusions about the association difficult. In such cases we use Cramer's V. SPSS computes both measures together, even when we are interested in one only.

Example

A study of 100 men and 100 women found that 23 men were in favour (Pro) and 77 against (Con) feminism; and 12 women were in favour and 88 against feminism. We shall use the Phi coefficient to test whether there is an association between 'gender' and 'attitudes to feminism'.

How to compute it

To compute the Phi coefficient we proceed as follows:

- Select **Analyze/Descriptive statistics** and click on **Crosstabs**.

- Transfer one variable to the **Row(s)** box; and one to the **Column(s)** box.

- Click on **Statistics** and activate **Phi and Cramer's V**.

- Click on **Continue**.

- Click **OK**.

Following this, the computer displays the output in the Viewer. The relevant figures are shown in the 'Symmetric Measures' table (see Figure 8.1).

Symmetric Measures		Value	Approx. Sig.
Nominal by Nominal	Phi	.145	.041
	Cramer's V	.145	.041
N of Valid Cases		200	

a. Not assuming the null hypothesis.

b. Using the asymptotic standard error assuming the null hypothesis.

Figure 8.1

What are we looking for?

We focus on...	We ask...
1 The value of phi	Does it indicate a strong, weak, or no correlation?
2 P-value	Is the p-value significant?

The information we need to address the correlation is in the 'Symmetric Measures' table.

Interpretation of Phi

We know already that a Phi value that is close to 1 indicates a strong association, and one close to 0 indicates a weak (or no) association. Given that the value of Phi is close to 0 (.145), we can argue that the association between gender and attitudes to feminism is very weak. Substantively speaking this means that being a male or a female does not imply that one is more or less in favour of feminism.

Similarly, a p-value that is less than significance level suggests a significant correlation, otherwise the correlation is not significant. The results show a p-value of .041, indicating that this association is statistically significant. This means that the probability that the association described above is due to error or chance is only 4 in 100.

Lambda coefficient (λ)

What is this?

Lambda is a measure that describes the extent to which one variable can predict another by computing the absolute proportional reduction of the prediction error, and is suitable for variables, of which at least one is nominal. There is a symmetric and an asymmetric measure.

Example

A study found that 40 males were religious and 56 nonreligious; and 89 women were religious and 18 nonreligious. Is there an association between gender and religiosity'

How to compute it

To compute the Lambda coefficient we proceed as follows:

- Select **Analyze/Descriptive statistics** and click on **Crosstabs**.
- Transfer one variable to **Row(s)** box and one to **Column(s)** box.

- Click **Statistics** and activate **Lambda**.

- Click **Continue**.

- Click **OK**.

The output displayed in the Viewer is given in Figure 8.2.

Gender * Religiousness Crosstabulation

Directional Measures

			Value	Asymp Std Error[a]	Approx T[b]	Approx Sign
Nominal by nominal	Lambda	Symmetric	318	084	3.301	.001
		Gender Dependent	396	070	4.646	.000
		Religiousness Dependent	216	117	1.644	.100
	Goodman & Kruskal tau	Gender Dependent	185	054		.000[c]
		Religiousness Dependent	185	054		.000[c]

a Not assuming the null hypothesis

b Using the asymptotic standard error assuming the null hypothesis

c Based on chi-square approximation

Figure 8.2

The logic of Lambda

For a symmetric test the question is: What is the *mutual predictability* between the variables? For an asymmetric test the question is: *How much* of the predicting error can be reduced by having knowledge of the independent variable? The answer to these questions is guided by a set of rules. First of all we know that Lambda values range from 0 to 1 (no negative values!). Apart from this we know that:

- A value of 0 suggests that the knowledge of the one variable cannot reduce the predicting error at all when estimating the other variable.

- A value of 1 indicates that knowledge of the one variable can reduce this error by 100 per cent.

- Values between 1 and 0 show by how much the predicting error can be reduced by knowing the other variable (eg .6 means 60 per cent, .3 means 30 per cent, etc).

What are we looking for?

We focus on...	We ask...
1 The value of Lambda (λ)	Does it indicate a strong, weak, or no correlation?
2 P-value	Is the p-value significant?

The main values we are looking for are Lambda, and then the p-value.

What do these figures mean?

The Viewer displayed three figures. These are the 'Symmetric' lambda; one for 'Gender Dependent'; and one for 'Religiousness Dependent'. The value for the symmetric lambda (.318) means that the *mutual predictability* of the variables is about 32 per cent. The figure .396 (rounded off to .4), being the value for *gender being the dependent variable* means that knowing a person's religiousness, can reduce 40 per cent of the predicting error when estimating this person's gender. The value for 'Religiousness Dependent' is .216, and means that knowing a person's gender, can reduce 21.6 per cent of the predicting error when estimating this person's religiousness.

Finally, the p values are very strong in the symmetric lambda (.001) and when gender is the dependent variable (.000), but weak when religiousness is the dependent variable (.100). Hence, while in the first two cases the associations are very significant and extremely significant respectively, in the third case the association is not significant.

Need more info?
Online statistics texts:

- HyperStat:http://davidmlane.com/hyperstat/index.html

- Stat Primer: http://www.sjsu.edu/faculty/gerstman/StatPrimer/

- StatSoft: http://www.statsoft.com/textbook/stathome.html

- StatNotes: www2.chass.ncsu.edu/garson/pa765/statnote.htm

CHAPTER 9

Correlation tests
For ordinal variables

We now move to association methods for ordinal variables. As with tests for nominal variables, the purpose of these tests is to examine whether ordinal variables are associated in some way and some degree. For instance, whether students who are ranked high in sport are also ranked high in academic performance.

As shown in Table 9.1, the tests which are usually employed in such cases are Gamma (γ), Somers' d, and Spearman's rho. We shall address these tests next, beginning with Gamma (γ).

Table 9.1 Which test do I use and when?

If your variables are	You use the test
Nominal	φ (phi) coefficient, Cramer's V or Lambda (λ)
Ordinal	Spearman's rho, Gamma (γ) or Somers' d
Interval/ratio	Pearson's r

Gamma (γ)

What is gamma?

Gamma is a measure of ordinal association, and is symmetric and suitable for tables of any size. It is used only with crosstabulated frequency distributions, and not if data are measured as continuous variables. Being symmetric, gamma helps to establish whether there is an association between the variables, without distinguishing between dependent and independent variables; it is nondirectional. Gamma is thought to be the most common measure of ordered crosstabular association.

Example

A study of the relationship between social class (lower, middle, upper class) and scholastic achievement (very high, high, low, very low achievement) has been conducted. We employ gamma to establish whether there is an association between the variables.

How to compute gamma

To compute gamma we proceed as follows:

- Select **Analyze/Descriptive statistics** and click on **Crosstabs**.

- Transfer **class** to Row(s) box and **achiev** to Column(s) box.

- Click on **Statistics** and activate **Gamma**.

- Click on **Continue**.

- Click **OK**.

Following this, the computer displays a number of tables, of which the one presented in Figure 9.1 is the most relevant.

Symmetric Measures				
	Value	Asymp. Std. Error[a]	Approx. T[b]	Approx. Sig.
Ordinal by Ordinal Gamma	1.000	.000	44.272	.000
N of Valid Cases	100			

a. Not assuming the null hypothesis.

b. Using the asymptotic standard error assuming the null hypothesis.

Figure 9.1

What are we looking for?

We focus on...	We ask...
1 The value of Gamma (γ)	Does it indicate a strong, weak, positive or negative correlation?
2 P-value	Is the p-value significant?

Gamma is interpreted according to its strength and direction. Being a symmetric measure, Gamma does not show which variable affects which; it rather focuses on the association between the variables in general.

What do the results mean?

The information we need to know is the value of gamma and the p-value. The results indicate that there is a very high and positive association (1.00) between the variables, and that the association is 'extremely significant' (.000).

Substantively speaking we can argue that high class status is associated with high achievement at school. Still the test does not specify which variable generates the association.

Need more info?
Online statistics texts:

- SticiGui Text: http://www.stat.berkeley.edu/~stark/SticiGui/Text/index.htm

- Statistics at square one: http://www.bmj.com/collections/statsbk/index.shtml

- CAST: http://cast.massey.ac.nz/

- Look for answers to questions: http://www.answers.com/

- Introductory Statistics: http://www.psychstat.missouristate.edu/sbk00.htm

Somers' d

What is this?

Somers' d is a measure for ordinal data. It is a measure based on concordant and discordant pairs and is suitable only for crosstabulated frequency distributions, and for tables of any size; it is also not employed if data are measured as continuous variables. Somers' d makes a computational and conceptual reference to independent and dependent variables, aiming to ascertain the extent to which the former affects the latter, and the direction of the effect.

Example

A study explored the question whether quality of friendships (Excellent, Good, Fair, Poor) affects life satisfaction (Very Satisfied, Satisfied, Unsatisfied, Very unsatisfied). We employ Somers' d to establish whether there is an association between the variables.

How to compute it

To compute Somers' d we proceed as follows:

- Select **Analyze/Descriptive statistics**.

- Click on **Crosstabs**.

- Transfer one variable to the **Row(s)** box and one to the **Column(s)** box.

- Click on **Statistics** and activate **Somers' d**.

- Click on **Continue**.

- Click **OK**.

Following this, the computer displays a number of tables, of which the one presented in Figure 9.2 is the most relevant.

Directional Measures

			Value	Asymp. Std. Error[a]	Approx. T[b]	Approx. Sig.
Ordinal by Ordinal	Somers' d	Symmetric	.557	.055	8.792	.000
		Life satisfaction Dependent	.541	.056	8.792	.000
		Quality of friendships Dependent	.576	.056	8.792	.000

a. Not assuming the null hypothesis.

b. Using the asymptotic standard error assuming the null hypothesis.

Figure 9.2

What are we looking for?

We focus on...	We ask...
1 The value of Somers' d	Does it indicate a strong, weak, positive or negative correlation?
2 P-value	Is the p-value significant?

Remember that Somers' d is interpreted according to its strength and direction. It further allows the researcher to estimate the ranking of the dependent variable from knowledge of the independent variable.

What do the results mean?

The value of Somers' d is .557, and the p-value is .000. This suggests that there is a substantial correlation between the two variables, and that the p-value is very high. Substantively speaking this means that the quality of friendships has a positive impact on life satisfaction.

Spearman's rho

What is this?

Spearman's rho is a product-moment, nonparametric correlation coefficient which deals with ranks (not magnitudes), and measures the strength of the linear association between two (ordinal) variables. Unlike other ordinal measures, this is a correlation-based measure.

Example

Fifteen students were ranked according to their participation in sport and their performance in examinations, using relevant scales. The results were entered in the computer. We now want to test whether there is an association between the two variables.

How to compute it

To compute Spearman's rho we proceed as follows:

- Select **Analyze/Correlate/Bivariate**.

- Transfer **Sport** and **Performance** to **Variable(s)** box.

- Activate **Spearman**, by clicking on the square box in front of it.

- Activate **Two-tailed** or **One-tailed**(*).

- Activate **Flag significant correlations**.

- Click **OK**.

(*) Note: 'One-tailed' is chosen if the direction of the correlation is known; if not, 'Two-tailed' is chosen.

The output displayed in the Viewer and the correlation table are shown in Figure 9.3.

What are we looking for?

We focus on...	We ask...
1 Spearman's rho value	Does it indicate a strong, weak, positive or negative correlation?
2 P-value	Is the p-value significant?

Correlations

			Sport Ranks	Performance Ranks
Spearman's rho	Sport Ranks	Correlation Coefficient	1.000	-.964
		Sig (2-tailed)	.	.000
		N	15	15
	Performance Ranks	Correlation Coefficient	-.964**	1.000
		Sig (2-tailed)	.000	.
		N	15	15

Figure 9.3

As noted above, the focus at this stage is exactly the same as in other correlation tests: the value of Spearman's rho and the p-value. The former is in the cell that lies in the intersection of the row for Sport Ranks and the column for Performance Ranks. The latter is given below Spearman's rho. The standards of evaluation of their values are the same as those discussed earlier when referring to other types of correlation tests.

What do the results mean?

Spearman's rho is -.964 and its p-value .000. Having established these values, we can assess the nature of association between the variables.

- A rho value of -.964 indicates that there is a very strong negative correlation between sport participation and school performance. This suggests that high ranks in sport participation are associated with low ranks in school performance.

- A p-value of .000 suggests that the correlation is 'extremely significant', or significant at the .001 level (see page 63).

CHAPTER 10

Correlation – regression
For interval/ratio variables

In this chapter we shall address one correlational method that assists data analysts with assessing associations between continuous variables, such as the amount of TV viewing (in hours) and years of age, or income and alcohol expenses.

As shown in Table 10.1, the test that is employed to test associations between interval/ratio variables is Pearson's r. This is a very common and popular test, is easy to compute and to interpret, and will be introduced next.

Table 10.1 Which test do I use and when?

If your variables are	You use the test
Nominal	φ (phi) coefficient, Cramer's V or Lambda (λ)
Ordinal	Spearman's rho, Gamma (γ) or Somers' d
Interval/ratio	Pearson's r

Pearson's correlation (r)

What is this?

Pearson's correlation is a symmetrical, interval/ratio level test, and deals with pairs of scores, and with magnitudes (not with ranks). It is used to test whether there is a linear association between two variables, and if so, whether this correlation is strong, weak, positive or negative.

Example

To check the relationship between test scores in mathematics and in social research (SR), the scores of ten students in these subjects were recorded. The results were entered in the computer. Pearson's r is used to check the relations between these variables.

Using scattergrams

It is useful and also advisable that before running this test, a scatter-gram is constructed. This is also a common practice among data analysts because it offers an overview of the nature of the relationship between the variables. Employing the procedure we explained in Chapter 5, we obtain the following graph.

The scattergram in Figure 10.1 shows a positive and rather strong correlation between Math-scores and SR-scores, meaning that students who are doing well in the one subject tend to be doing well also in the other. Let us now see whether Pearson's coefficient corroborates this finding.

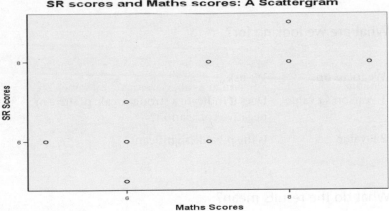

Figure 10.1

Computing Pearson's r

To compute Pearson's coefficient we proceed as follows:

- Select **Analyze/Correlate** and click **Bivariate**.
- Transfer **Math-Scores** and **SR-Scores** to **Variables** box.
- Activate first **Pearson**, and then **Two-tailed**.
- Activate **Flag significant correlations** and click **OK**.

The results are shown in Figure 10.2.

Correlations

		Math-Scores	SR-Scores
Math-Scores	Pearson Correlation	1	.750*
	Sig. (2-tailed)		.013
	N	10	10
SR-Scores	Pearson Correlation	.750*	1
	Sig. (2-tailed)	.013	
	N	10	10

*. Correlation is significant at the 0.05 level (2-tailed).

Figure 10.2

What are we looking for?

We focus on...	We ask...
1 Pearson's r value	Does it indicate a strong, weak, positive or negative correlation?
2 P-value	Is the p-value significant?

What do the results mean?

- In our example, the r is .750 (or .75), which indicates that the correlation between Math-scores and SR-scores is strong.
- The correlation is positive. This suggests that changes in one variable (eg performance in maths) are followed by changes in the other variable in the same direction. In other words, the higher the performance in maths, the higher the performance in social research.

- The p-value is .013, which means that the relationship is significant at the .05 level. This is also shown in the value of r which is marked by a single asterisk (.750*).

This answers fully the research question.

Partial correlation

What is this?

This is a procedure employed to test the correlation between two variables when the presence of an intervening variable is suspected. If there are reasons for this, analysts 'control' for (or 'partial out') the variable that is thought to interfere, and explore further the correlation between the original variables.

Example

As shown in the previous section, there is a strong significant correlation between Math-Scores and in SR-Scores. Now we want to see whether this correlation is genuine or the outcome of other variables, such as the students' overall performance (OverPerf-Scores). It is quite possible that high performance in SR is the result of students' overall scholastic ability rather than their performance in mathematics. Partial correlation will assist with explaining this relationship.

How to compute it

To conduct partial correlation we proceed as follows:

- Select **Analyze/Correlate/Partial**.
- Transfer **Math-Scores** and **SR-Scores** to **Variables** box.
- Transfer **OverPerf-Scores** to **Controlling for** box.
- Click **OK**.

The results displayed in the output are shown in Figure 10.3.

Correlations

Control Variables			Math-Scores	SR-Scores
OverPerf-Scores	Math-Scores	Correlation	1.000	-.179
		Significance (2-tailed)	.	.645
		df	0	7
	SR-Scores	Correlation	-.179	1.000
		Significance (2-tailed)	.645	.
		df	7	0

Figure 10.3

What are we looking for?

We focus on...	We ask...
1 Correlation value	Does it indicate a strong, weak, positive or negative correlation?
2 P-value	Is the p-value significant?

What do the results mean?

The figures in the Correlation table show that the correlation coefficient is very low (-.179), almost negligible, and negative; they show also that the association is not significant (.645). In other words, there is no significant association between Math-Scores and SR-Scores when overall performance is controlled for.

This shows also that the initial correlation of .750 between scores in maths and in social research declined significantly to -.179 when controlling for 'overall performance'. Taking it a step further and putting it in a more general context, one could assume that obtaining good scores in social research may not be associated primarily with students' mathematical skills but rather with their overall ability to do well in their studies.

Simple regression

What is this?

Regression is also known as 'prediction'. It is the technique of estimating the extent to which the dependent variable (criterion variable) will change if the independent variable (predictor variable) changes by one unit. It is a method that allows prediction of one variable when another is known, and is suitable mainly for quantitative variables measured at the ordinal, interval or ratio level.

Decisive for the estimation of regression is the *slope* (displayed as **B** or **b**) and the *intercept* (displayed as **a**). The slope is also known as the *unstandardized regression coefficient* and intercept as the *constant*. There are many types of regression. *Simple regression, multiple regression, hierarchical regression* and *logistic regression* are a few examples.

Example

A school survey addressed the question whether reading time can predict school performance, in other words, the more students read, the better their performance score, and vice versa. The hours spent by 15 students reading and their performance scores were used to test the relationship.

How to compute it

To compute the regression analysis for the above example we proceed as follows:

- Select **Analyze/Regression** and click on **Linear**.
- Transfer **School performance** to **Dependent** box.
- Transfer **Reading time** to **Independent(s)** box.
- Set **Method** to **Enter** (if not already set) and click **OK**.

Following this, the output is displayed in the Viewer containing four tables of which two – 'Model summary' and 'Coefficients' – are most relevant. These tables are shown in Figure 10.4.

Model Summary

Model	R	R Square	Adjusted R Square	Std. Error of the Estimate
1	.986(a)	.972	.969	.287

a Predictors: (Constant), Reading time

Coefficients^a

Model		Unstandardised Coefficients		Standardized Coefficients	t	Sig.
		B	Std. Error	Beta		
1	(Constant)	.312	.286		1.092	.295
	Reading time	.619	.029	.986	21.066	.000

a Dependent Variable: School performance

Figure 10.4

What are we looking for?

The points we focus on are:

a) The value of the *Regression Coefficient* for 'reading time' in the Coefficient table; its value is .619.

b) The *R* which is .986 (see Model Summary table in Figure 10.4).

c) The value of *Adjusted R square* (see Model Summary table in Figure 10.4), which is .969. This displays the amount of variance that can be explained by the regression model.

d) The p-value.

What do the results mean?

1 The value .619 of the regression coefficient indicates that when reading time increases by one unit, school performance increases by .619 units; the p-value is .000, which is the highest level possible. Substantively speaking this means that the amount of reading time is a good predictor of school performance.

2   The value of R, being .986 suggests that the correlation between the variables is very strong and positive.

3   Finally, the value of Adjusted R Square, which is .969, suggests that the regression model explains about 97% of the variance in school performance.

These figures reinforce the assumption described above, regarding reading time as a good predictor of school performance.

Remember!
As in the case of correlation, you can start your computation with a scatterplot. This offers a quick overview of the nature of the relationship between the variables. The way you obtain a scatterplot was explained in Chapter 2.

Multiple regression

What is this?

Multiple regression is a method that tests the relationship between two or more independent variables and one dependent variable. In this sense, this is an extension of simple regression. While in simple regression we asked whether 'reading time' can predict school performance, in multiple regression we can add a second predictor, eg sport involvement (in hours), and examine the power of the model to predict school performance. Let us explore this example.

How to compute it

To compute multiple regression analysis for the above example we proceed as follows:

- Select **Analyze/Regression** and click on **Linear**.

- Transfer **School performance** to the **Dependent** box.

- Transfer **Sport participation** and **Reading time** to **Independent(s)** box.

- In the **Method** box select option **Enter** (if not already chosen).

- Click **OK**.

Following this, the Viewer displays four tables of which the following are the most relevant, shown in Figure 10.5. (Note that in the 'Method' box there are several options to consider, eg Enter, Stepwise, Forward, Backward and Remove. We chose 'Enter'. The other options are beyond the scope of this book.)

Model Summary

Model	R	R Square	Adjusted R Square	Std. Error of the Estimate
1	.990[a]	.979	.976	.255

a Predictors: (Constant), Sport involvement, Reading time

Coefficients[a]

Model		Unstandardized Coefficients		Standardized Coefficients		
		B	Std. Error	Beta	t	Sig.
1	(Constant)	2.778	1.190		2.335	.038
	Reading time	.448	.085	.713	5.273	.000
	Sport involvement	-.082	.038	-.287	-2.121	.050

a Dependent Variable: School performance

Figure 10.5

What are we looking for?

The most decisive points, and those directly related to prediction are those listed below.

1 **B values:** B values are listed in the B column of the Coefficients table and correspond to the independent variables (IVs). They state by

how much the dependent variable (DV) will change if the IV changes by one unit.

2   **Standardized coefficients:** these are the values contained in the Beta column of the Coefficients table. They show the overall impact each IV has on the DV, and allow conclusions as to which of the IVs has the strongest impact on the DV.

3   **R:** the value of R, which is in the 'Model Summary table', tells us whether there is a correlation between the IVs and the DV, and if so whether this is strong, weak, positive or negative, and more so how this coefficient compares to that of the correlation with a single independent variable.

4   **Adjusted R Square:** this is in the Model Summary table, and represents the coefficient of multiple determination, which shows how much of the variance in the DV can be explained by the regression model.

Interpretation: what do they mean?

There are four conclusions we can draw from these results:

1   The B values tell us that if reading time is increased by one unit, school performance will increase by .448 units; and if sport involvement is increased by one unit, school performance will decrease by .082 units (-.082). Note that both values are statistically significant.

2   The values of the standardized coefficients tell us that, of the two IVs, reading time has a stronger impact on school performance than sport involvement (.713 vs. -.287).

3   The value of R demonstrates that the correlation between the IVs and the DV is very strong (.990) and also slightly stronger than when reading time was the only IV (.990 vs. .986).

4   The Adjusted R Square shows that the model explains about 98 percent (.976) of variation in the DV, and this is slightly stronger than when reading time was the only IV (.969).

All relevant questions have been answered.

Useful concepts

Alternative hypothesis (H_1) A hypothesis about a population parameter that reflects the research hypothesis.

Asymmetric measures of association Measures whose value is contingent upon which variable is set to be the independent and which the dependent.

Bias A systematic error in planning or executing research.

Bivariate analysis An analytic procedure including two variables.

CADA Abbreviation for Computer assisted data analysis.

Category A group of people of the same or similar attributes.

Causality The state of a relationship between variables where the one causes changes in the other.

Coding The process of transforming raw data into numbers for the purpose of analysis.

Constant An attribute that does not change.

Continuous variable A variable that can be subdivided into a large and often infinite number of sub-units; eg 'Age' expressed in 'Years' with months, weeks, days, hours, etc. covering the space between them. A person can be 25 years, 6 months and 18 hours old.

Data Numerical figures reflecting the raw material gathered in a research study.

Dependent variable A variable which is set to be explained or affected by another.

Dichotomous variable A variable which contains two values.

Discrete variable A variable containing distinct attributes with no continuity between them, eg 'Gender', containing 'Males' and 'Females', with no alternative options between them.

Hypothesis testing A procedure employed to test whether or not sample data were generated by chance.

Independent variable A variable which is set to affect another variable.

Inference The practice of generalizing evidence produced by sample research.

Interval/ratio measurement A type of measurement that employs intervals of equal distance.

Interval variable A variable measured using interval measurement.

Mean The sum of all scores, divided by their number (the average).

Median The score that divides a ranked distribution into two equal parts.

Mode The category of a distribution that has the highest number of cases.

Multivariate analysis An analytic procedure including more than two variables.

Nominal measurement This entails naming the category of a variable to which a case belongs.

Nominal scale A scale in which items can only be defined as equal or unequal, same or different.

Non-parametric test A test that does not assume normality of the population, is appropriate for nominal and ordinal level data, and does not compare means.

Null hypothesis (H_0) A hypothesis that states the opposite of the research hypothesis and which is expected to be rejected.

One-tailed tests Those tests in which the region of rejection is on one 'tail' of the sampling distribution and which are directional.

Ordinal measurement A measurement format that ranks the values of a variable.

Ordinal scale A scale in which items are arranged according to their relationship to each other.

p-value The significance of test results computed by a test. In SPSS: 'Asymp. Sig', or 'Sig'.

Parameters Descriptive attributes relating to populations.

Parametric tests Tests based on the assumption that the population from which samples have been taken is normally distributed; suitable for interval/ratio level.

Population A group of similar research subjects, which is the focus of a study, from which a sample is taken, and to which the sample results are to be generalized.

Range A measure of dispersion, which is the difference between the largest and the smallest score of the distribution.

Ratio measurement Interval measurement including also a zero.

Related sample A sample that contains the same subjects (eg when tested twice using a before–after measurement), or when subjects are matched, also known as matched or dependent samples.

Reliability The capacity of an instrument to produce consistent results.

Representativeness The capacity of a sample to stand for the research population.

Sample The group of research units selected from a population to be studied.

Secondary analysis An analysis of data previously collected and processed by another study.

Significance An attribute reflecting the validity of the findings. Differences can be significant or not significant; they are significant if the findings reflect differences in the population, and are not caused by errors or by chance.

Significance level The probability of obtaining a statistic by chance or error.

Significance tests Significance tests compare frequency counts or means, relating to one, two or more variables. They compare probabilities with significance levels. There are two types of significance tests: the parametric and nonparametric tests.

Standard deviation A measure of dispersion, which is the square root of variance.

Statistics Numerical attributes relating samples.

Symmetric measures of association Measures whose value remains the same, regardless of which variable is the dependent and which the independent.

Two-tailed tests Those tests in which the region of rejection falls within both tails of the sampling distribution and which are non-directional.

Units of analysis The people, objects or phenomena that constitute the objects of research.

Univariate analysis A mode of analysis containing one variable at a time.

Unrelated sample A sample that contains different and unrelated subjects, or subjects that are not matched, also known as independent samples.

Validity A property of a research instrument which measures its relevance, precision and accuracy.

Variables An empirical construct that can take more than one value.

Variance A measure of dispersion, signifying the average of the squared deviations from the mean.

Verification The process of empirical validation, mainly of hypotheses.

Index

DATE DUE
